EVEN MORE TRUE STORIES

An Intermediate Reader

by Sandra Heyer

Longman

Introduction

EVEN MORE TRUE STORIES is an intermediate reader for students of English as a Second Language. It consists of 15 units centered around high-interest stories adapted from newspapers and magazines. The vocabulary and structures used in the stories are carefully controlled to match those of a typical intermediate ESL course. At the same time all attempts have been made to keep the language natural.

PRE-READING

A photograph introduces each unit. Pre-reading activities beneath the photo are suggested to motivate the students to read, to encourage predictions about the content of the reading, and to prompt students to share knowledge and experiences related to the topic.

READING THE STORY

Some students might find it helpful to first skim the story by reading the first paragraph and the first sentences of subsequent paragraphs. Students who have a tendency to stop at each unfamiliar word should be encouraged to read silently twice, once without stopping, and then again, stopping to circle new vocabulary.

When all the students have finished reading, the teacher clarifies new vocabulary. If the students read at home, they use the vocabulary exercises to help clarify new words. If time permits, the teacher may wish to read the selection aloud while the students follow along in their texts.

Teachers might also point out organizational devices used in the stories, such as introductory anecdotes, topic sentences, transitions, and conclusions.

Teachers should, of course, adapt whatever reading strategies best suit their classes.

THE EXERCISES

Each unit offers a variety of post-reading exercises. Both the choice and use of the exercises are flexible and will depend on the individual teaching environment and style. Students can work individually, in pairs, or in small groups. The exercises can be completed in class or assigned as homework. The perforated answer key at the back of the book affords the teacher a choice in the method of correcting the exercises.

Vocabulary. The vocabulary exercises are designed to aid comprehension by helping define unfamiliar words. The unfamiliar words in each story were identified by students who participated in field-testing the stories. The words that most students designated as "new" and that could be clearly explained were included in the exercises.

Looking at the Story encourages guessing meaning through contextual clues. Some exercises are multiple choice, some are fill-in-the-blank, and some are "or" questions based on the text.

Looking at a New Context is the supplemental vocabulary exercise in some units. The first part of the exercise serves as a model for the second part. The examples in the first part were provided by ESL students. The second part can be done in a number of ways. For students who do not have enough experience with English to make their own examples, this part works best as a teacher-led exercise. The teacher gives an example of each word in a new context (Be careful not to say the new words!), and students try to guess which word the teacher is describing. (A tip: To keep students alert, use their names in your examples. Say, for instance, "When Elena cuts paper, she uses a . . . .") Write each word on a flashcard and show it to the students after they have guessed the word. Most intermediate-level students can complete this part unsupervised in small groups if they are permitted to look at the word list. The most advanced students will be able to work independently in groups and guess the words without referring to their textbooks.

Looking at Special Expressions is the supplemental vocabulary exercise in other units. Because idiomatic expressions are best clarified through a combination of definition and example, the definition of each expression is followed by a matching exercise which offers three examples of the expression in use.

Comprehension. The comprehension exercises are not intended to test the students' understanding of the reading as much as to introduce reading skills that will foster comprehension.

Understanding the Main Ideas is a multiple-choice exercise. In one type of exercise, the students circle the correct information; in another type, they draw a line through the information that is not in the story. The latter exercise is a subtle introduction to outlining; what remains after the incorrect information is crossed out is an outline of the story.

Understanding Supporting Details is a matching exercise. As students match main ideas with "examples," they learn to identify supporting details.

Understanding Details recycles some of the vocabulary from the vocabulary exercises, verifies comprehension, and encourages the development of scanning techniques.

Scanning for Information helps students learn to scan quickly for names, dates, place names, and numbers. It provides practice in a skill that university-bound students in particular need.

Understanding Cause and Effect focuses the students' attention on relationships expressed by the word *because*.

Understanding Time Relationships helps students establish the sequence in which information or events are reported.

Discussion and Writing. Two spin-off exercises end each unit. A discussion exercise asks students to personalize the ideas and themes presented in the reading by discussing questions with classmates, sharing opinions, and exchanging information about their respective countries. Many of the discussion exercises require students first to complete an activity in pairs or small groups so that all students—even those in large classes—have a chance to participate. It is hoped that these discussions will provide further pleasure from the reading process and give insights into cultural similarities and differences.

The final exercise is a guided writing based on the reading. The examples are the work of intermediate-level ESL students.

The expanded exercise section in EVEN MORE TRUE STORIES is not meant to suggest that the exercises are more important than the story itself; it simply offers the teacher greater flexibility in meeting the sometimes divergent needs of intermediate-level students. Both the stories and exercises in EVEN MORE TRUE STORIES are intended to offer pleasure in reading and to stimulate the students' imagination and interest in things incredible but true.

Contents

1. PRE-READING

Look at the picture and think about these questions. Discuss your answers with your classmates.

■ The girl in the picture is named Lizzie. What kind of a girl do you think Lizzie is? Do you think she does what her parents want her to do? Do you think she usually behaves or misbehaves?

■ If you guessed that Lizzie often misbehaves, you were right. She threw her mother's wedding ring into the toilet and put ice cream into the VCR. She is a brat. (*Brat* is not a polite word.)

■ In this story you will read about Lizzie and other brats. Have you ever known any brats? What did they do when they misbehaved?

Brats

A FEW years ago a French toy company had an unusual contest—a "biggest brat" contest. The company had a prize for the child whose behavior was the worst in the world. Over 2,000 parents entered their children in the contest. "Our child is the world's biggest brat!" they wrote. The parents made lists of all the bad things their children had done. Judges read the lists and chose the winner. She was a little girl from the United States. Her name was Lizzie, and she was four years old. Here are a few of the things Lizzie did to win the title, "The World's Biggest Brat":

- She put a garden hose into the gas tank of her father's car. Then she turned on the water.
- She painted a leather sofa with spray paint.
- She threw her mother's wedding ring into the toilet. Then she flushed the toilet.
- She put an ice cream sandwich into the VCR.
- She set the table for dinner. Then she glued the silverware to the table. Imagine her parents' surprise when they sat down to eat and tried to pick up their forks!

Lizzie may be the world's biggest brat, but she is certainly not the world's only brat. Alo is a five-year-old boy from Bangladesh. One afternoon, while his father was asleep on the sofa, Alo cut off his father's mustache. A few days later, he cut off his brother's eyebrows when his brother was sleeping in the bedroom. A few weeks after that, he cut off most of his mother's hair when she was asleep at night. Alo's family now keeps every pair of scissors under lock and key and always sleeps behind locked doors.

The behavior of a Mexican boy named Manuel is perhaps even worse than Lizzie's and Alo's because it is more dangerous. Manuel likes to play with matches. One day he found some matches near the kitchen stove. He took the matches, sneaked into his parents' bedroom, and set fire to the curtains. Fortunately, Manuel's mother walked into the bedroom just in time. She pulled down the curtains and put out the fire before it spread.

Hiroshi, a young Japanese man, says that he rarely misbehaved when he was a young child but turned into a real brat when he was about 13. "My friends and I used to sneak around at night and let the air out of tires. We were terrible," he says. "Our parents tried to control us, but they didn't have much success. We drove them crazy."

No mother or father wants to be the parent of a brat. Parents everywhere try to control their children's behavior. Some parents spank their children when they misbehave. Other parents won't let their children watch TV or eat dessert. In Japan, parents often send their children outside when they misbehave and tell them they can't come into the house. In the United States, parents do just the opposite: they send their children to their bedrooms and tell them they can't go outside.

Lizzie's parents don't know what to do about Lizzie. Her mother says, "I keep telling myself that Lizzie is going through a stage, but sometimes I don't know. . . It seems like she's always getting into trouble." Lizzie's father says, "One day we'll look back on all this and laugh."

What does Lizzie think about her behavior? Lizzie doesn't like to talk about it. When a reporter asked Lizzie if she was "a bad girl," Lizzie kicked his leg. Then she yelled, "I'm not a brat! I'm an angel! Get out of my house!"

2. VOCABULARY

A. LOOKING AT THE STORY

Think about the story and answer the questions.

1. When people win *prizes*, are they usually happy or sad?

    They are usually happy.

2. What goes through a garden *hose*—electricity or water?

    _____

3. What are made of *leather*—blouses or shoes?

    _____

4. If you *glue* two things, do they stay together or do they stay apart?

    _____

5. Is *silverware* knives, forks, and spoons, or is it rings, earrings, and necklaces?

    _____

6. Does a man with a *mustache* have hair on his arms or on his face?

    _____

7. Do *scissors* cut or write?

    _____

8. When Manuel *sneaked* into his parents' bedroom, did he walk quietly or noisily?

    _____

9. Are *curtains* on windows or on beds?

    _____

10. Manuel's mother said, "*Fortunately*, I walked into the bedroom just in time." Did she think, "I had bad luck" or did she think, "I had good luck"?

    _____

11. Jenny misbehaves every day. Mary misbehaves only once or twice a month. Which girl *rarely* misbehaves?

    _____

12. Do people *kick* with their hands or with their feet?

    _____

B. LOOKING AT A NEW CONTEXT

Read the sentences. Then write the correct word on the line.

leather   kick   fortunately

1. I ate lunch at a restaurant. When the waitress brought the check, I discovered that I had left my money at home. _____, a friend of mine was at the restaurant, too. He lent me the money to pay for my lunch.

2. When I play soccer, I hit the ball with my head, or I _____ the ball with my feet.

3. I went shopping to buy a new belt. I saw two belts. They looked similar, but one belt was $5, and the other belt was $30. I didn't understand why the one belt was so much more expensive. Then I saw that the cheaper belt was made of plastic, and the more expensive belt was made of _____.

Now make your own examples for the new words:

prize	leather	silverware	scissors	curtains	rarely
hose	glue	mustache	sneak	fortunately	kick

First, form small groups. One student in each group is the "teacher." The "teacher" will write each word on a separate small piece of paper, fold the papers, and give one to each person in the group. The "teacher" will take a word, too. Hold your paper so that no one can see your word. Make up a little story for your word like the ones above. (Be careful not to say your word.) Your classmates will listen to your story and try to guess which word you have. Then listen to your classmates' stories and try to guess which words they have.

3. COMPREHENSION/READING SKILLS

A. UNDERSTANDING THE MAIN IDEAS

What information is *not* in the story? Draw a line through the information.

1. The winner of the "biggest brat" contest
   a. was named Lizzie.
   b. was four years old.
   c. was from the United States.
   d. had blond hair.

2. Lizzie
   a. filled the gas tank of her father's car with water.
   b. drew pictures on the living room wall.
   c. painted a leather sofa with spray paint.
   d. flushed her mother's wedding ring down the toilet.

3. Some other brats are
   a. Alo, who cut off his family's hair.
   b. Marie, who hits other children.
   c. Manuel, who plays with matches.
   d. Hiroshi, who used to let air out of tires.

4. Parents try to control their children's behavior by
   a. making them stand in a corner.
   b. spanking them.
   c. not letting them watch TV or eat dessert.
   d. sending them outside or to their bedrooms.

B. UNDERSTANDING DETAILS

Read the following sentences. One word in each sentence is not correct. Find the word and cross it out. Write the correct word.

1. A few years ago a ~~Korean~~ *French* toy company had an unusual contest.

2. The company wanted to find the child whose behavior was the best in the world.

3. Over 200 parents entered their children in the contest.

4. The parents made lists of all the good things their children had done.

5. The winner of the contest was a little boy from the United States.

Now copy three sentences from the story, but change one word in each sentence so that the information is not correct. Give your sentences to a classmate. Your classmate will find the incorrect word in each sentence, cross it out, and write the correct word. When your classmate is finished, check the corrections.

6. _____

_____

7. _____

_____

8. _____

_____

4. DISCUSSION

A. Think about these questions. Discuss your answers with your classmates.

1. When you were a child, were you a "brat" sometimes or were you always an "angel"? Can you remember anything bad you did? Tell your classmates about it.
2. What do you think about spanking children who misbehave?
3. Do you know a child who often misbehaves? What bad things does the child do?
4. Do you think children in different countries behave differently? Or do you think children everywhere behave the same way?

B. Imagine that you are a parent in the following situations. In small groups, read about each problem and decide what you would do. Circle the answers your group chooses, or write your own answers.

1. When you return home from shopping with your son, you discover a small toy in his pocket. He has stolen the toy from a department store. You
   a. spank him and send him to his room.
   b. let him keep the toy this time.
   c. go back to the store with him and return the toy.
   d. _____

2. You tell your teenage daughter to be home by 10 P.M. She wants to stay out later. As she leaves the house, she yells, "I hate living here!" and slams the door. You

   a. run after her to tell her that she has to stay home.
   b. run after her to tell her she must come back and leave the house again quietly.
   c. do nothing.

   d. _____

3. You are at a department store with your three-year-old daughter. She wants you to buy her a toy; you say, "No." She lies down on the floor and screams. You

   a. pick her up and carry her out of the store.
   b. buy her the toy.
   c. explain to her why she can't have the toy.

   d. _____

4. Your six-year-old son comes home crying. An older boy in the neighborhood has hit him. You

   a. tell the older boy never to hit your son again.
   b. talk to the older boy's parents.
   c. give your son karate lessons.

   d. _____

5. WRITING

Answer one of the questions from Discussion Exercise 4A in writing. Here is what one student wrote.

I remember something bad I did when I was in school. Our school was made of adobe—that's dried mud—and the walls were soft. My seat was next to a wall. One day I was bored and I pushed my pencil into the wall. It made a small hole. The next day I pushed my pencil into the hole again and made the hole deeper. Every day I pushed my pencil deeper and deeper into the hole. Finally my pencil went through the wall. Then I began making another hole. I was busy making holes in the wall for days. Then the teacher noticed the holes. She was very angry and moved my seat away from the wall. That was the end of hole-making, and I was bored again.

Now answer one of the questions in writing.

UNIT 2

1. PRE-READING

Find a partner. With your partner, make a list of things that you or your partner uses
every day.

Here are some examples:

    comb   key   TV   bed   spoon

- Do not list clothes or things you use up, like food or toothpaste. In three minutes, try to make the longest list in the class.
- Do you think about the things you use every day? The man in the picture does. He says that our "everyday things" often give us trouble. In the next story, you will learn why.

Trouble with Everyday Things

JANE couldn't watch her favorite TV programs because she worked in a restaurant at night. She decided to buy a VCR so that the VCR could record the TV programs while she worked. Then she could watch them when she came home.

Jane was excited the day she bought her VCR. She hurried home from the store and, after an hour's work, finally succeeded in connecting the VCR to the TV. Then she tried to program the VCR to record a TV program. Two hours later she was still trying. Jane didn't figure out how to program her VCR that day, or the next day. In fact, she never figured out how to program her VCR. "I'm just not good with machines," she thought.

Jane blamed herself when she couldn't program her VCR. Donald Norman says she shouldn't have. He has a degree in electrical engineering and uses a multi-million-dollar computer at work, and he can't figure out his VCR either. He is the author of *The Design of Everyday Things*. In his book Dr. Norman says that if people have trouble with the things they use every day—VCRs, stoves, watches, doors—they shouldn't blame themselves. Instead, they should blame the design of these "everyday things."

The modern stove, for example, is an everyday thing with a poor design. Most stoves in the United States look like this:

The four burners form a square, but the knobs form a line. That's a bad design, says Dr. Norman. That's why people often turn on the wrong burner, even though the knobs are labeled. A better design might look like this:

The burners form a square, so the knobs form a square, too. It's easier to see which knob controls each burner. "Why can't all stoves be like this?" Dr. Norman asks.

Another everyday thing with a confusing design is the digital watch. In the past, watches simply told the time; now watches often have as many as 15 different features. They beep on the hour and show the day and date; some even tell the temperature. Can people really figure out how to use all those features? Dr. Norman says that a lot of people can't. The problem, he says, is that generally only three buttons control all the features on a digital watch. That design means trouble.

Simple things like doors sometimes have confusing designs, too. Have you ever had trouble opening a door? Have you ever pushed on a door that pulls open, or pulled on a door that pushes open? When you have trouble opening a door, it's probably because the door is poorly designed. Well-designed doors tell people exactly what to do. A door with a handle tells people to pull; a door with a bar tells people to push. If you're pulling at a door that pushes open, the door probably has a handle on it. The door is giving you the wrong signal. It has a bad design.

What should people do about all these everyday things that are poorly designed? "Don't buy them!" Dr. Norman says. If you're shopping for a VCR, ask the salesperson if you can try to program it right in the store. If you can't program that VCR, keep shopping until you find one you can program. And don't buy something just because it looks good. Washing machines, for example, often look impressive. Their control panels have a dozen buttons to push and dials to turn; they look like they came from a spaceship. The washing machines look great, but can you figure out how to work them? If people continue to buy poorly designed products, Dr. Norman says, companies will continue to make them—and people will continue to have trouble with everyday things.

2. VOCABULARY

A. LOOKING AT THE STORY

Read the sentences. Then complete the statements below each. Circle the letter of the correct answer.

Jane finally succeeded in *connecting* the VCR to the TV, but she never *figured out* how to program the VCR. She *blamed* herself when she couldn't program her VCR.

1. Machines that are connected look like this:

 a.   b.

2. To "figure out" means to
   a. cut.   **b.** understand.

3. When she blamed herself, Jane thought,
   a. "I'm not good with machines. I'm responsible for this problem."   **b.** "I understand machines very well. I can solve this problem."

Donald Norman uses a *multi-million*-dollar computer at work and is the *author* of *The Design of Everyday Things*.

4. A multi-million-dollar computer costs
   a. less than a million dollars.   **b.** more than a million dollars.

5. An author is a person who
   a. writes books.   **b.** paints pictures.

The modern stove is an everyday thing with a poor design. The four *burners* form a square, but the *knobs* form a line. People often turn on the wrong burner, even though the knobs are *labeled*.

6. A burner is

   a.   b.

7. A knob is something you find on
   a. machines and doors. You turn it, and something happens.   **b.** books and magazines. You read it, and something happens.

8. A label tells people
   a. what something is.   **b.** what time it is.

Another everyday thing with a *confusing* design is the digital watch. Watches often have as many as 15 different *features*. They beep on the hour and show the day and date; some even tell the temperature.

9. "Confusing" means
   a. easy to understand.   **b.** difficult to understand.

10. Which watch has more features?

a.

b.

Don't buy something *just* because it looks good. Washing machines often look *impressive*. Their control panels have a dozen buttons to push and dials to turn; they look like they came from a spaceship.

11. "Just" sometimes means

    a. and.   **b.** only.

12. When you see something that you think is impressive, you say,

    a. "Wow! That's good!"   **b.** "I don't like this."

B. LOOKING AT A NEW CONTEXT

Read the sentences. Then write the correct word on the line.

    blamed   just   connected

1. I made a cake and put it in the oven. Then I wanted to sleep for an hour, so I told my

husband, "Watch the cake." When I woke up, I smelled something burning. I looked in

the oven, and my cake was black. "You didn't watch the cake!" I said to my husband. I

_____ him for the burned cake.

2. I put a tape into the VCR, turned on the VCR and the TV, and pushed "play." Nothing

happened. Then I saw that the TV and the VCR weren't _____.

3. I wasn't hungry, so when the waitress came to take my order, I said,

"_____ coffee, please."

Now make your own examples for these words:

connect	multi-million	knob	features
figure out	author	label	just
blame	burner	confusing	impressive

First, form small groups of students. One student in each group will be the "teacher." The "teacher" will write each word on a separate small piece of paper, fold the papers, and give one to each person in the group. The "teacher" will take a word, too. Hold your paper so that nobody can see your word. Make up a little story for your word like the ones above. (Be careful not to say your word.) Your classmates will listen to your story and try to guess which word you have. Then listen to your classmates' stories and try to guess which words they have.

3. COMPREHENSION/READING SKILLS

A. UNDERSTANDING THE MAIN IDEAS

What information is *not* in the story? Draw a line through the information.

1. Jane
   a. bought a VCR to record TV programs while she worked.
   b. succeeded in connecting the VCR to the TV after an hour's work.
   c. never figured out how to program her VCR.
   d. ~~has worked in a restaurant for 11 years.~~

2. Donald Norman
   a. has a degree in electrical engineering.
   b. uses a multi-million-dollar computer at work.
   c. has two VCRs.
   d. is the author of *The Design of Everyday Things*.

3. Examples of everyday things with poor designs are:
   a. most stoves in the United States.
   b. microwave ovens.
   c. digital watches.
   d. some doors.

4. Most stoves in the United States have
   a. clocks that beep on the hour.
   b. four burners that form a square.
   c. four knobs that form a line.
   d. poor designs.

5. Digital watches have
   a. as many as 15 different features.
   b. three buttons that control all the features.
   c. confusing designs.
   d. small batteries.

6. A well-designed door
   a. has the word "EXIT" on it.
   b. tells people exactly what to do.
   c. pulls open if it has a handle.
   d. pushes open if it has a bar.

7. Dr. Norman gives this advice:
   a. Don't buy everyday things that are poorly designed.
   b. Buy everyday things only if they're on sale.
   c. Try to program a new VCR right in the store.
   d. Don't buy something just because it looks good.

B. UNDERSTANDING CAUSE AND EFFECT

Find the best way to complete each sentence. Write the letter of your answer on the line.

1. __C__ Jane thought she wasn't good with machines

2. _____ People often turn on the wrong burner

3. _____ A lot of people can't figure out how to use all the features on their digital watches

4. _____ People sometimes pull on a door that pushes open

a. because their stoves are poorly designed; the burners form a square, and the knobs form a line.

b. because it has a handle.

c. because she couldn't figure out how to program her VCR.

d. because only three buttons control all the features.

4. DISCUSSION

A. Dr. Norman says that digital watches often have confusing designs. Is that true? Do an experiment. Find one person in your class who knows how to set his or her digital watch. Find another person who has no experience with digital watches. Ask the person with the watch to teach the other person how to set the watch so that the alarm goes off in five minutes. Can they do it?

B. Compare designs of everyday things in your native country and in the country where you are living now, for example:

stove	bed	public telephone (pay phone)
refrigerator	window in a home	light switch
shower and bathtub	student desk	electrical plug and outlet
toilet	telephone in a home	mailbox

With a partner or in a small group, describe or draw the everyday things that have different designs in your native country.

5. WRITING

Write a riddle. Describe an everyday thing in as many sentences as you can. Write your description so that your classmates cannot guess what the everyday thing is until they hear the last sentence. For example:

- It's round.
- It usually has holes in it.
- It's often white, but it can be other colors, too.
- It's usually made of plastic, but it can be made of metal, wood, or other materials.
- It's not expensive.
- Almost everyone in the world has more than one.
- My shirt has nine of them.

What is it? (Answer: a button)

Now write your sentences. When you are finished, read your riddle to your classmates. They will try to guess what the everyday thing is.

UNIT 3

1. PRE-READING

Compare gestures in your native country with gestures in other countries. Your teacher will ask you the questions below. Answer the questions using only your hands. Do not speak! As you answer each question, look at your classmates. Which gestures are the same? Which gestures are different?

In your native country how do you say . . . ?

1. Come here.
2. Go away.
3. I can't hear you.
4. You have a phone call.
5. Who, me?

6. Yes.
7. No.
8. I don't know.
9. Wait a minute.
10. He/She's crazy.

11. He/She's intelligent.
12. Money
13. A long time ago
14. This is good.
15. This is bad.

More Alike Than Different

EVERYONE listened attentively as the woman spoke.

"If you want to say 'OK,' don't make a circle with your thumb and first finger," the woman began. "That means OK here in the United States, but in the Soviet Union it's an obscene gesture."

The audience of 300 Americans chuckled; a few people took notes.

"It's all right to admire something," the woman continued, "but don't be too enthusiastic. Don't say, 'I *really* like your tablecloth.' Your Soviet friend will offer you the tablecloth and will be offended if you don't take it.

"Remember that, in general, life in the Soviet Union is not as comfortable as life in the United States. You might not have hot running water, or you might have to share a bathroom with five or six people."

The woman was preparing the Americans for their trip to the Soviet Union. In the Soviet Union, the language, customs, and food would be different. Even simple things, like making a phone call, would be different. The Americans wanted to learn about these differences before their trip. They didn't want to experience culture shock.

When they arrived in the Soviet Union, the Americans were glad that they had prepared for their trip. Most of them experienced only a little culture shock. They enjoyed their visit and made a lot of Soviet friends.

Making friends was, in fact, the purpose of the trip. The trip was planned by The Friendship Force, an international organization that promotes world peace. The Friendship Force believes that people who are friends will not fight wars. So, to help people from all over the world become friends, it organizes exchanges of people. The U.S.–Soviet exchange was the largest exchange that it has ever organized. In April 1990, 300 Americans visited the Soviet Union, and 300 Soviets visited the United States.

The Soviets, like the Americans, prepared for their visit by learning about life in the other country. Still, they, too, experienced a little culture shock.

The Soviets knew that Americans were fond of pets, but they were shocked to see pets inside homes. They couldn't believe their eyes when they saw dogs eating in the kitchen and sleeping on people's beds.

They were surprised at the difference between everyday life in the Soviet Union and in the United States. The Americans' lives, they said, were much easier. A Soviet woman gasped when she saw an American pour rice directly from a box into a pan of boiling water. "You didn't wash the rice?" she asked. She explained that at home she had to wash the rice carefully and pick out all the stones. "Are you kidding?" the American said. "If people here had to do that, nobody would buy rice."

The Soviets knew that Americans liked to eat fast food in restaurants, but they were disappointed to see that Americans ate fast meals at home, too. In the Soviet Union, the evening meal often lasts an hour or two because families sit at the table and talk. When American families eat together—*if* they eat together—they often eat quickly and don't take time for long conversations. The Soviets thought that was a shame.

In spite of their differences in language and culture, the Soviets and Americans became friends. The two women in the picture became friends, even though the Soviet woman couldn't speak a word of English and the American woman couldn't speak a word of Russian. For two weeks they communicated through sign language and dictionaries.

Some of the Americans who traveled to the Soviet Union were schoolchildren from a sixth-grade class. When they returned to the United States, their teacher asked them to write about their trip. One 11-year-old girl wrote, "I have learned a lot from this experience. I learned to adapt to a different culture. And I learned that people all over the world are more alike than they are different."

2. VOCABULARY

A. LOOKING AT THE STORY

Read the following sentences. Then complete the statements. Circle the letter of the correct answer.

Everyone listened *attentively* as the woman spoke.

1. To listen attentively is to listen
   a. carefully.
   b. nervously.

"Don't make a circle with your thumb and first finger," the woman said. "That's an *obscene* gesture in the Soviet Union." The *audience* of 300 Americans *chuckled*.

2. An obscene gesture is
   a. not polite.
   b. polite.

3. An audience
   a. listens or watches.
   b. sings, dances, or speaks.

4. To chuckle is to
   a. sing loudly.
   b. laugh quietly.

"It's all right to *admire* something," the woman said, "but don't be too *enthusiastic*. Don't say, 'I really like your tablecloth.' Your Soviet friend will offer you the tablecloth and will be *offended* if you don't take it."

5. If you admire something, you
   a. don't like it.
   b. like it.

6. If you are enthusiastic, you are
   a. interested and excited.
   b. bored and tired.

7. People who are offended are
   a. a little angry because their feelings are hurt.
   b. a little nervous because they don't know what to do.

The Soviets knew that Americans were *fond of* pets.

8. People who are fond of pets
   a. don't like pets.
   b. like pets.

A Soviet woman *gasped* when she saw an American pour rice directly from a box into a pan of boiling water. "You didn't wash the rice?" she asked.

9. People gasp when they are
   a. tired.
   b. surprised.

The Soviets knew that Americans liked to eat fast food in restaurants, but they were *disappointed* to see that Americans ate fast meals at home, too.

10. People who are disappointed are
    a. not happy.
    b. happy.

An 11-year-old girl wrote, "I learned to *adapt* to a new culture. And I learned that people all over the world are more *alike* than they are different."

11. People who adapt
    a. don't change.   **b.** change.

12. "Alike" means
    a. the same.   **b.** strange.

B. LOOKING AT A NEW CONTEXT

Read the sentences. Then write the correct word on the line.

enthusiastic   alike   disappointed

1. Last year I went to a beach hotel for my vacation. I thought I would have a wonderful time, but I had a terrible time. It rained every day, and the people at the hotel weren't friendly. I was _____.

2. My friend loves classical music. I had two tickets for a classical music concert, so I asked her if she wanted to go with me. "Yes!" she answered. "That concert will be great!" She was _____ about the concert.

3. I have a sister who is one year older than I am. My sister is a good student, and I am, too. My sister likes to sew, and I do, too. My sister has a cat, and I do, too. My friends tell me, "You and your sister are so much _____."

Now make your own examples for the new words:

attentively	chuckle	offended	disappointed
obscene	admire	fond of	adapt
audience	enthusiastic	gasp	alike

First, form small groups. One student in each group is the "teacher." The "teacher" will write each word on a separate small piece of paper, fold the papers, and give one to each person in the group. The "teacher" will take a word, too. Hold your paper so that no one can see your word. Make up a little story for your word like the ones above. (Be careful not to say your word.) Your classmates will listen to your story and try to guess which word you have. Then listen to your classmates' stories and try to guess which words they have.

3. COMPREHENSION/READING SKILLS

A. UNDERSTANDING THE MAIN IDEAS

Circle the letter of the best answer.

1. "More Alike Than Different" is about
    a. the language, customs, and food in the Soviet Union.
    b. a U.S.–Soviet exchange of people that was organized by The Friendship Force.
    c. communicating through sign language and dictionaries.

(Continued on next page.)

2. The Friendship Force is
   a. an international organization that promotes world peace.
   b. an organization that prepares Americans for visiting the Soviet Union.
   c. an international organization of children who visit other countries.

3. The Friendship Force believes that
   a. people who live in the Soviet Union do not have comfortable lives.
   b. people who are friends will not fight wars.
   c. people who do not speak English will experience culture shock in the United States.

4. To help people become friends, The Friendship Force
   a. sends language teachers all over the world.
   b. mails letters all over the world.
   c. organizes exchanges of people.

5. The Americans prepared for their visit by
   a. experiencing culture shock.
   b. writing essays.
   c. learning about Soviet life.

6. The Soviets who visited the United States were shocked to see
   a. Americans eating rice.
   b. pets in people's homes.
   c. fast-food restaurants.

7. Although their languages and cultures were different, the Soviets and the Americans
   a. ate the same food.
   b. became friends.
   c. had the same everyday lives.

B. UNDERSTANDING SUPPORTING DETAILS

Find the best way to complete each sentence. Write the letter of your answer on the line.

1. _____ "It's all right to admire something, but don't be too enthusiastic. For example,

2. _____ The Friendship Force organizes exchanges of people. For example,

3. _____ The Soviets were shocked to see pets inside homes. For example,

4. _____ The Soviets said that the Americans' lives were much easier than theirs. For example,

5. _____ In spite of their differences in language and culture, the Soviets and Americans became friends. For example,

a. they couldn't believe their eyes when they saw dogs eating in the kitchen.

b. the two women in the picture became friends, even though the Soviet woman couldn't speak English and the American woman couldn't speak Russian.

c. don't say, 'I *really* like your tablecloth.'"

d. Soviets have to wash their rice carefully, but Americans don't.

e. in 1990 The Friendship Force sent 300 Americans to the Soviet Union and 300 Soviets to the United States.

4. DISCUSSION

A. Have you ever had a bad, embarrassing, or funny experience in a foreign country because you didn't know the customs? Tell your classmates about it.

B. When people move to a new country, they often go through three stages. These are the stages:

Stage 1: Arrival
- Everything is new and different
- Happy, excited

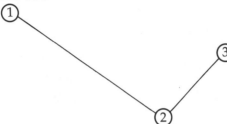

Stage 3: One to two years after arrival
- Can speak new language, understand customs, laugh at mistakes
- Adapted, feel "at home"

Stage 2: Six weeks to six months after arrival
- Everything in native country is better
- Sad, want to go home

Are you in a new country? If so, where are you—at stage 1, stage 2, stage 3, or somewhere in between? Put an X to show where you are. Then show a classmate where you put your X. Tell your classmate why you put your X where you did.

5. WRITING

Imagine that The Friendship Force is sending a group of people to your native country. What might surprise the visitors? Prepare the visitors so that they don't experience culture shock. Here is what one student wrote.

Be careful when you shop in Syria. The prices you see in store windows are sometimes not the actual prices. For example, you might see a pair of shoes in a store window. Next to the shoes is the price. But when you go into the store, you find out that the real price of the shoes is more than the price in the window. So, Syrians don't always believe the prices they see in store windows. If people from other countries believe those prices, they will have a bad surprise.

Now write about your native country. Prepare visitors so that they don't experience culture shock.

UNIT 4

1. PRE-READING

Look at the picture and think about these questions. Discuss your answers with your classmates.

- Do you come from a large family? Do your classmates come from large families? How many brothers and sisters do they have? Which classmate comes from the largest family?
- Your family or your classmate's family may be large, but it is not as large as the family of the man and woman in the picture. They have the world's largest family. They are the parents of 53 children.

The World's Largest Family

MR. and Mrs. Albina don't know where all their grown children are living now. Some of them, they know, are in Argentina, but they aren't sure where in Argentina. They aren't sure how old all their children are, either. Ask them, for example, "How old is your daughter Susanna?" and they say, "We're not sure." They might even say, "Which Susanna?" But it is understandable that the Albinas can't keep track of their children's addresses and ages. After all, they have 53 children.

Mr. and Mrs. Albina, with 53 children, have the world's largest family. Not one of their children is adopted.

When people hear about the Albinas' large family, the first question they ask is, "How is it possible? How can one woman give birth to 53 children in her lifetime?" The answer is simple: Every time Mrs. Albina gave birth, she had twins or triplets. She was a triplet herself; she thinks that's why she always had twins or triplets.

The Albinas married when Mrs. Albina was 12 years old and Mr. Albina was 30. The children came quickly, in twos and threes. The first 21 children were boys. Mrs. Albina loved her sons, but she wanted a daughter very much.

The Albinas spent the early years of their marriage in Argentina. Then they decided to move to Chile. To travel from Argentina to Chile, they had to cross the Andes Mountains. Mr. and Mrs. Albina and their 21 sons made the difficult, two-week journey on mules. One night there was a terrible snowstorm in the mountains. During the snowstorm, Mrs. Albina gave birth to triplets, a boy and—two girls! Mrs. Albina now has 16 more girls, including twins who are 15 months old.

The oldest Albina children are in their thirties and forties. They are on their own now, but 18 of the Albina children still live with their parents. The family lives in a two-room shack in Colina, Chile. The shack has electricity but no toilet or running water. The children wash in a small bowl in the dusty backyard.

At times there is very little food in the Albinas' small house. When there is not enough food for everyone, Mrs. Albina makes sure the youngest children do not go hungry. "The smallest eat first, and then the bigger ones. We've always done it that way," she says. Obviously, the Albinas do not have enough money for their big family. Why, then, do they continue to have children?

The Albinas do not use birth control because it is against their religion. They could let other people take care of their children, but Mrs. Albina will not allow it. "When my two brothers and I were babies," she says, "our mother left us at an orphanage and never returned. We lived there together until we were five. Then a couple adopted my brothers, and I was left behind. I was heartbroken. I promised myself that when I became a mother, I would never give my children away. Even if I didn't have much money, I would always take care of my children myself." Mrs. Albina has kept her promise.

So, the Albina family continues to grow. Mr. and Mrs. Albina have so many children that they ran out of names for them all and had to give some children the same name. There are three Susannas, three Miriams, two Estrellas, and two Soledades.

Will there be a fourth Susanna or a third Estrella? Will the Albinas stop at 53 children, or will there be more? Mr. Albina is 77 years old, and Mrs. Albina is 59. "I'm getting old," she says with a smile. "I would like God to think of me and consider my age. But, if God sends more children to me, yes, there will be more."

2. VOCABULARY

A. LOOKING AT THE STORY

Think about the story and answer the questions.

1. Are *grown* children babies or adults?

   _____

2. When a woman gives birth to *triplets*, how many children are born at the same time?

   _____

3. Is a *journey* a long trip or a short trip?

   _____

4. Who are the parents of a *mule*—a horse and a donkey, or a dog and a wolf?

   _____

5. Is a *shack* small and roughly built or large and well built?

   _____

6. Is something that is *obvious* easy to see or difficult to see?

   _____

7. Birth control is *against* the Albinas' religion. Does their religion permit birth control, or does it not permit birth control?

   _____

8. Is an *orphanage* a home for children who are sick or for children who have no parents?

   _____

9. Did the couple who *adopted* Mrs. Albina's brothers take the boys into their family or leave them at the orphanage?

   _____

10. Mrs. Albina wants God to *consider* her age. Does she want God to forget her age or think about her age?

    _____

B. LOOKING AT SPECIAL EXPRESSIONS

Find the best way to complete each sentence. Write the letter of your answer on the line.

to keep track of = to remember; to keep a record of

1. _*c*_ The Albinas can't

2. _____ He uses a small notebook to

3. _____ Could I use your telephone? I'll

a. keep track of my long-distance calls and pay you for them later.

b. keep track of his expenses.

c. keep track of their children's addresses and ages.

after all = it must be remembered

4. _____ It is understandable that the Albinas aren't sure where all their children are. After all,

5. _____ I'm not surprised they did well on the English test. After all,

6. _____ I know she hasn't finished the work, but after all,

to run out of = to have no more

7. _____ Mr. and Mrs. Albina have so many children that

8. _____ I can't make the cake because

9. _____ He couldn't finish the test because

d. they've studied English for over six years.

e. she's very busy.

f. they have 53 children.

g. he ran out of time.

h. they ran out of names for them all.

i. I've run out of flour.

3. COMPREHENSION/READING SKILLS

A. UNDERSTANDING THE MAIN IDEAS

Circle the letter of the best answer.

1. How many people are in the world's largest family?
   a. 55: a mother, a father, and their 53 adopted children
   b. 23: a mother, a father, and their 21 sons
   c. 55: a mother, a father, and their 53 children

2. All of the Albina children are
   a. living in Argentina.
   b. in their thirties and forties.
   c. twins or triplets.

3. The Albina family is
   a. rich.
   b. middle class.
   c. poor.

4. The Albinas do not use birth control because
   a. they want to have as many children as possible.
   b. they don't know about birth control.
   c. it is against their religion.

5. Mrs. Albina will not let other people take care of her children because
   a. she is afraid other people won't take good care of them.
   b. she promised that she would always take care of her children herself.
   c. she has a lot of money and can take care of them herself.

6. Will the Albinas have more children?
   a. Yes.
   b. No.
   c. Maybe.

B. SCANNING FOR INFORMATION

The underlined information is not correct. Find the correct information in the story and write it. Work quickly; try to complete this exercise in three minutes or less.

1. The Albinas married when Mrs. Albina was 12 years old and Mr. Albina was 29. *30*

2. The first 24 children were boys. *2*

3. The Albinas spent the early years of their marriage in Peru. *Argent.*

4. Then they decided to move to Bolivia. *Chile*

5. The Albinas and their sons made the three-week journey across the Andes Mountains *two* on mules.

6. During a snowstorm Mrs. Albina gave birth to twins. *triplets*

7. Mrs. Albina now has 14 more girls. *16*

8. The Albinas live in a two-room shack in Santiago, Chile. *Colina*

9. Mrs. Albinas and her brothers lived together at the orphanage until they were four. *5*

10. There are two Miriams. *3*

4. DISCUSSION

A. First answer the questions yourself. Then ask a classmate the questions. Talk over the answers with your classmate.

	YOU	YOUR CLASSMATE
1. How many brothers and sisters does your mother have?		
2. How many brothers and sisters does your father have?		
3. How many brothers and sisters do you have?		
4. If you are married: How many children do you have? If you are not married: Do you want to have children someday? How many?		
5. How many children are in the ideal family? (Is one child best? Two children? Five children?)		
6. How many children do most families in your country have today?		
7. Are families in your country getting bigger or smaller?		
8. Does your country have too many people?		
9. Does the government try to control population in your country?		

Now work as a class and answer the following questions.

1. Which classmate has the most aunts and uncles?
2. Which classmate has, or wants to have, the most children?
3. Do your classmates agree on the number of children in the ideal family?
4. In which countries are families getting bigger? Getting smaller? Staying the same size?
5. Which countries have too many people?

B. Talk about your family with a partner. First, take a piece of paper. On the paper, draw a square for each person in your family. Do not draw inside the squares. Now imagine that your paper is a page from a photo album and that each square is a photo of someone in your family. Show your "album" to your partner. Tell your partner about each person in your family. Then listen while your partner describes the people in his or her family.

5. WRITING

Write about your family or your partner's family. Here is what one student wrote.

I came from a traditional family in Taiwan. There are six people in my family: my parents, an older brother, and two older sisters. I'm the youngest.

My father started his own company 25 years ago. He's going to retire at the end of this Chinese year. I hope he'll be able to relax and enjoy life a little more then. My mother is a traditional Chinese housewife. I think she is one of the reasons my father has been successful. She has always taken care of our home so that my father could concentrate on his career. My two sisters are both in Japan now; one is married to a Japanese man, and the other studies at a music college in Tokyo. My brother is a swimming coach at a private health club. My brother and I are good friends.

My family, I guess, is ordinary but means a lot to me.

Now write about your family or your classmate's family.

UNIT 5

1. PRE-READING

Look at the picture and think about these questions. Discuss your answers with your classmates.

- The fish have needles in their backs. Have you ever seen needles like these? What are they used for?
- Why do you think the fish have needles in their backs?

Healthy Again

MR. Cho was worried. Something was wrong with his goldfish. They had red patches on their skin, they weren't eating, and they didn't have much energy. Mr. Cho thought the fish probably had an infection. To cure the infection, he stuck needles into the backs of the fishes. That may seem unusual to some people, but it didn't seem unusual to Mr. Cho. Mr. Cho is an acupuncturist—a person who uses needles to treat illness and pain.

Mr. Cho left the needles in the fish for several minutes and then took them out. During the next few days he repeated the treatments. Soon the fish began to feel better. They swam with more energy and started to eat again, and the red patches on their skin disappeared. Did the fish get better because of the acupuncture treatments? Mr. Cho thinks so.

Although acupuncture for goldfish is uncommon, acupuncture for people is very common in Asia. Acupuncturists there help people who have medical problems like infections, backaches, and stomachaches. They even use acupuncture during operations so that patients don't feel pain.

To see what happens during an acupuncture treatment, let's imagine that Ming, a man who often has headaches, decides to go to Dr. Han, an acupuncturist. This is what might happen at Dr. Han's office.

First Dr. Han examines Ming and asks him about his headaches. There are many kinds of headaches, and Dr. Han needs to know what kind of headaches Ming has.

Then Dr. Han decides where to insert the needles. Ming is surprised when Dr. Han tells him that she will insert needles in his neck and foot, but none in his head. That is not unusual. Often acupuncture needles are not inserted in the place where the patient feels pain.

Next, Dr. Han chooses the needles, which range in size from one-half inch long to six inches. Dr. Han chooses one-inch needles for Ming and begins to insert them. Ming feels a little pinch when each needle goes in. That is not unusual, either. Some patients say it hurts a little when the needles go in; other patients say it doesn't hurt at all. The needles stay in place for 15 minutes. Then Dr. Han removes them. Before he goes home, Ming makes an appointment to see Dr. Han in a week. Dr. Han says that Ming will know in a few weeks if the treatments are working.

Acupuncture has helped millions of people, not only in Asia, but all over the world. People say that acupuncture works. But *how* does it work?

One explanation of how acupuncture works is thousands of years old. The ancient Chinese, who were the first to use acupuncture, believed that energy flowed through the human body. They thought that sometimes too much energy—or too little energy—flowed to one part of the body. That caused pain or sickness. There were, however, several hundred places on the body where an acupuncturist could change the flow of energy. Those places were called acupuncture points. A needle inserted into an acupuncture point on a patient's leg, for example, changed the flow of energy to the patient's stomach. When the energy flowed correctly again, the patient would feel better.

There is also a modern explanation of how acupuncture works. Scientists point out that the acupuncture points have many more nerve endings than other places on the skin. Nerve endings receive pain messages when someone is sick or hurt. The pain messages then travel through the nerves. Perhaps acupuncture also sends messages through the nerves. These messages interrupt pain messages that are on their way to the brain. Because the pain messages never reach the brain, the patient feels better.

People who have been helped by acupuncture probably don't care which explanation is correct. They are just happy to be like Mr. Cho's fish—healthy again.

2. VOCABULARY

A. LOOKING AT THE STORY

Which words have the same meaning as the words in the story? Circle the letter of the correct answer.

1. The fish had red *patches* on their skin.
   - **a.** places that looked different from the area around them
   - **b.** places where acupuncturists insert needles

2. Mr. Cho wanted to *cure the infection.*
   - **a.** learn about the fish
   - **b.** make the sickness go away

3. He *stuck* needles into the backs of the fishes.
   - **a.** threw
   - **b.** pushed

4. An acupuncturist is a person who uses needles to *treat* illness and pain.
   - **a.** try to cure
   - **b.** cause

5. During the next few days he *repeated the treatments.*
   - **a.** watched his fish very carefully
   - **b.** stuck needles into the backs of the fishes again

6. Acupuncture for fish is *uncommon.*
   - **a.** difficult
   - **b.** unusual

7. Dr. Han decides where to *insert* the needles.
   - **a.** put in
   - **b.** buy

8. The needles range in size from one-half inch long to six inches.
   - **a.** The smallest needles are one-half inch, the largest are six inches, and there are other sizes in between.
   - **b.** The needles come in two sizes, one-half inch and six inches.

9. The ancient Chinese believed that energy *flowed* through the human body.
   - **a.** escaped
   - **b.** ran like a river

10. These messages *interrupt* pain messages that are on their way to the brain.
    - **a.** stop
    - **b.** help

B. LOOKING AT SPECIAL EXPRESSIONS

Find the best way to complete each sentence. Write the letter of your answer on the line.

to point out = to draw attention to; to say "Look at this" or "Think about this"

1. _____ Scientists point out that acupuncture points
   - **a.** arrived in Chicago in the middle of the night.

2. _____ He pointed out that the bus we wanted to take
   - **b.** were missing from the Answer Key.

3. _____ The students pointed out that the answers for Unit 9
   - **c.** have many more nerve endings than other places on the skin.

3. COMPREHENSION/READING SKILLS

A. UNDERSTANDING THE MAIN IDEAS

What information is *not* in the story? Draw a line through the information.

1. What was wrong with Mr. Cho's goldfish?
   a. They had red patches on their skin.
   b. They weren't eating.
   c. ~~They had fevers.~~
   d. They didn't have much energy.

2. After the acupuncture treatments, Mr. Cho's fish
   a. swam with more energy.
   b. started to eat again.
   c. were sold for a lot of money.
   d. didn't have red patches on their skin anymore.

3. Acupuncturists in Asia use acupuncture
   a. to help people with backaches.
   b. to help people stop smoking.
   c. to help people with stomachaches.
   d. during operations so that patients don't feel pain.

4. What happened before Dr. Han inserted the needles?
   a. She told Ming how much the treatment would cost.
   b. She examined Ming and asked him about his headaches.
   c. She decided where to insert the needles.
   d. She chose one-inch needles.

5. What happened during Ming's acupuncture treatment?
   a. Dr. Han inserted the needles.
   b. Ming felt a little pinch when each needle went in.
   c. Ming walked around the office.
   d. The needles stayed in place for 15 minutes.

6. What are some explanations of how acupuncture works?
   a. It corrects the energy flow in the body.
   b. It interrupts pain messages on their way to the brain.
   c. It changes the flow of blood through the body.

B. UNDERSTANDING SUPPORTING DETAILS

Find the best way to complete each sentence. Write the letter of your answer on the line.

1. _____ Something was wrong with Mr. Cho's goldfish. For example,

2. _____ The fish began to feel better. For example,

3. _____ Acupuncture for people is very common in Asia. For example,

4. _____ There were several hundred places on the body where an acupuncturist could change the flow of energy. For example,

a. acupuncturists there use acupuncture during operations so that patients don't feel pain.

b. a needle inserted into an acupuncture point on a patient's leg changed the flow of energy to the patient's stomach.

c. they swam with more energy and started to eat again.

d. they had red patches on their skin and they weren't eating.

4. DISCUSSION

A. Think about these questions. Discuss your answers with your classmates.

1. Do you think Mr. Cho's fish got better because of the acupuncture treatments?
2. Have you ever had a sick pet? What did you do? Some people take their sick pets to animal doctors. The pets get medicine and sometimes operations. What do you think about that?
3. Have you ever had an acupuncture treatment? If you have, tell your classmates about it. If you've never had an acupuncture treatment, would you try it?

B. Acupuncture is one type of medicine. There are many other types of medicine, too. Look at the seven types of medicine below. Each type of medicine has a treatment for headache. Read about the treatments. If you had headaches often, which types of medicine would you try? For each type of medicine, check (✓) "yes" or "no." Then ask a classmate, "Would you try it?" Ask about each type of medicine and check "yes" or "no." If your classmate answers "no," ask, "Why not?"

Type of Medicine	Common Treatment for Headache	Would you try it?			
		YOU		YOUR CLASSMATE	
		Yes	No	Yes	No
1. Acupuncture	Insert one needle in the neck and another in the foot.				
2. Acupressure (also called Shiatsu)	With your fingertips, push on the back of the head and the sides of the forehead. Massage the hand between the thumb and the first finger.				

		YOU		YOUR CLASSMATE	
		Yes	No	Yes	No
3. Chiropractic	Give a massage; move the bones in the spine so that the spine is straight.				
4. Herbalism	Make tea by boiling a special plant or root. Give the tea to the patient, or give a pill made from the plant or root.				
5. Holistic Health Care	Treat not only the headache, but also mental or emotional problems that could be causing your headache.				
6. Spiritual Healing	Pray and put your hands on the person's forehead.				
7. Traditional Western Medicine	Give painkillers.				

Now work as a class and discuss these questions.

- Has anyone in the class tried these types of medicine? • What was the medical problem?
- Did the treatment work?

5. WRITING

A. Imagine that you receive a letter from a friend. Your friend writes you that he has a medical problem and is going to try acupuncture. Your friend is afraid because he has never had an acupuncture treatment and doesn't know what will happen. Write a letter to your friend. Tell your friend what happens during an acupuncture treatment.

B. Have you ever needed medical treatment? What was the problem? Which type of medicine did you choose? What happened during the treatments? Did you get better? Write about your experience. Here is what one student wrote.

A few years ago I had a painful shoulder and decided to try acupuncture. Before I tried acupuncture, I was afraid of it. I thought, "That looks painful!" When I saw the long needles, I thought they would run through my body. But I was wrong. The needles were long, but the acupuncturist didn't insert the whole needle. He found the place where my shoulder hurt and inserted 30 needles. He inserted the needles little by little, and I didn't feel any pain. I went to the acupuncturist for about a month. After that, my shoulder was better.

Now write about your experience.

UNIT 6

1. PRE-READING

Look at the picture and think about these questions. Discuss your answers with your classmates.

- What do you see in the picture? What do you think happened?
- The picture was taken at Pompeii. Where is Pompeii? Do you know what happened there? Tell your classmates what you know.

The Buried City

EVERY year thousands of tourists visit Pompeii, Italy. They see the sights that Pompeii is famous for—its stadiums and theaters, its shops and restaurants. The tourists do not, however, see Pompeii's people. They do not see them because Pompeii has no people. No one has lived in Pompeii for almost 2,000 years.

Once Pompeii was a busy city of 22,000 people. It lay at the foot of Mount Vesuvius, a grass-covered volcano. Mount Vesuvius had not erupted for centuries, so the people of Pompeii felt safe. But they were not safe.

In August of the year 79 Mount Vesuvius erupted. The entire top of the mountain exploded, and a huge black cloud rose into the air. Soon stones and hot ash began to fall on Pompeii. Then came a cloud of poisonous gas. When the eruption ended two days later, Pompeii was buried under 20 feet of stones and ash. Almost all of its people were dead.

Among the dead was a rich man named Diomedes. When the volcano erupted, Diomedes decided not to leave his home. The streets were filled with people who were running and screaming. Diomedes was probably afraid that he and his family would be crushed by the crowd. So, Diomedes, his family, and their servants—16 people all together—took some food and went down to the basement. For hours they waited in the dark, hoping the eruption would end. Then they began to cough. Poisonous gas from the mountain was filling the city. Diomedes realized that they had to leave. He took the key to the door, and a servant picked up a lantern. Together they walked upstairs. But the poisonous gas was already filling the house. When they were a few feet from the door, Diomedes and his servant fell to the floor and died. The 14 people downstairs died embracing one another.

For centuries Diomedes and his family lay buried under stones and ash. Then, in the year 1861, an Italian archeologist named Giuseppe Fiorelli began to uncover Pompeii. Slowly, carefully, Fiorelli and his men dug. The city they found looked almost the same as it had looked in the year 79. There were streets and fountains, houses and shops. There was a stadium with 20,000 seats. Perhaps most important of all, there were many everyday objects. These everyday objects tell us a great deal about the people who lived in Pompeii.

Many glasses and jars had a dark blue stain in the bottom, so we know that the people of Pompeii liked wine. They liked bread, too; metal bread pans were in every bakery. In one bakery oven there were 81 round, flat loaves of bread—a type of bread that is still sold in Italy today. Tiny boxes filled with a dark, shiny powder tell us that the women liked to wear eye makeup, and the jewelry tells us that pearls were popular in the year 79. Graffiti is everywhere in Pompeii. On one wall someone wrote "Romula loves Staphyclus." On another wall someone wrote "Everyone writes on these walls—except me."

Fiorelli's discoveries tell us much about the way the people lived. They also tell us much about the way they died.

One day Fiorelli was helping his men dig. When he tapped on the hard ash, he heard a hollow sound. He suspected that the space beneath was empty. As an experiment, he drilled a few holes in the ash and poured liquid plaster down the holes. When the plaster was hard, Fiorelli cleared away the ash. He found the plaster form of a man. The man's body had turned to dust long ago, but the ash had hardened around the space where the body had been.

During the next years Fiorelli filled dozens of spaces with plaster. The plaster forms show how the people of Pompeii looked in their last moments of life. Some have calm expressions on their faces; others look very afraid. Some people died holding their children. Others died holding gold coins or jewelry. Diomedes died with a silver key in his right hand, and his servant died holding a lantern.

Giuseppe Fiorelli, too, has died, but his work continues. One-fourth of Pompeii has not been uncovered yet. Archeologists are still digging, still making discoveries that draw the tourists to Pompeii.

2. VOCABULARY

A. LOOKING AT THE STORY

Which words or picture has the same meaning as the words in the story? Circle the letter of the correct answer.

1. Pompeii was *buried under* 20 feet of stones and ash.
   a. covered by
   b. hit by

2. Diomedes, his family, and their *servants* went down to the basement.
   a. the people who worked in their home
   b. the people who visited Pompeii

3. A servant picked up a *lantern*.
   a. light
   b. knife

4. The 14 people downstairs died *embracing one another*.
   a. holding one another
   b. arguing with one another

5. Slowly, carefully, Fiorelli and his men *dug*.
   a.
   b.

6. There were streets and *fountains*, houses and shops.
   a.
   b.

7. There was a *stadium* with 20,000 seats.
   a. large indoor theater
   b. large sports field with rows of seats around it

8. There were also everyday *objects* that tell us a great deal about the people who lived in Pompeii.
   a. ideas
   b. things

9. There were many glasses and jars with a dark blue *stain* in the bottom.
   a. juice made from purple grapes
   b. spot that can't be removed

10. *Graffiti* is everywhere in Pompeii.
    a. writing on the walls
    b. garbage

11. When he *tapped on* the hard ash, he heard a hollow sound.
    a. hit lightly
    b. listened to

12. He *suspected that* the space beneath was empty.
    a. told everyone that
    b. thought that probably

B. LOOKING AT A NEW CONTEXT

Read the sentences. Then write the correct word on the line.

embraced   suspected   lanterns

1. A girl was waiting for her boyfriend. He arrived an hour late. He smelled of perfume

   and had lipstick marks on his face. She _____ that he had another

   girlfriend.

2. When my brother was in the army, he was away for one year. On the day he came

   home, my whole family went to the train station to meet him. When he got off the train,

   we all _____ him.

3. In my native country, people who live in the cities have electric lights. But in some places

   in the country, there is no electricity, and the people use _____.

Now make your own examples for these words:

bury	fountains	lantern	objects
servants	stain	embrace	tap
dig/dug	graffiti	stadium	suspect

First, form small groups. One student in each group is the "teacher." The "teacher" will write each word on a separate small piece of paper, fold the papers, and give one to each person in the group. The "teacher" will take a word, too. Make up a little story for your word like the ones above. (Be careful not to say your word.) Your classmates will listen to your story and try to guess which word you have. Then listen to your classmates' stories and try to guess which words they have.

3. COMPREHENSION/READING SKILLS

A. UNDERSTANDING CAUSE AND EFFECT

Find the best way to complete each sentence. Write the letter of your answer on the line.

1. _____ Tourists do not see Pompeii's people

2. _____ The people of Pompeii felt safe

3. _____ Diomedes decided not to leave his house

4. _____ We know that the people of Pompeii liked bread

5. _____ Fiorelli suspected that spaces beneath the ash were empty

a. because he was afraid that he and his family would be crushed by the crowd.

b. because he heard a hollow sound when he tapped on the ash.

c. because Pompeii has no people.

d. because Mount Vesuvius had not erupted for centuries.

e. because Fiorelli found metal bread pans in every bakery.

B. UNDERSTANDING TIME RELATIONSHIPS

"The Buried City" describes Pompeii at three different times: around the year 79, in the 1860s, and today. Read the sentences from the story. Decide what time the sentence tells about. Put a check (✔) in the right column.

	79	1860s	TODAY
1. Pompeii was a busy city of 22,000 people.	✔		
2. Tourists see the sights Pompeii is famous for, but they do not see its people.			
3. Mount Vesuvius erupted.			
4. Giuseppe Fiorelli began to uncover the city.			
5. Jewelry made of pearls was popular.			
6. Diomedes, his servants, and his family died.			
7. Fiorelli poured liquid plaster down the holes in the ash.			
8. Someone wrote "Romula loves Staphyclus" on a wall.			
9. Poisonous gas from the mountain filled the city.			
10. One-fourth of Pompeii is not yet uncovered.			

4. DISCUSSION

A. Think about these questions. Discuss your answers with your classmates.

1. Have you ever seen a volcanic eruption? Tell your classmates about it. Are there any volcanos in your native country? Where are they? Do they erupt sometimes?
2. The people of Pompeii lived at the foot of a volcano. That was a dangerous place to live. What cities today are in dangerous places? Why do people live there?
3. Do you know any other places that archeologists have uncovered or are still uncovering? Tell your classmates about them.

B. When the volcano erupted at Pompeii, people who left took their most important possessions. Imagine that your home is on fire. Everyone who lives with you is safe, but your home will burn to the ground. There is time for you to save three of your possessions. Which possessions will you save?

I will save

1. _____

2. _____

3. _____

Why are the possessions on your list important? Are they expensive? Were they gifts from special people? Are they things you can't buy? Show your list to a classmate. Explain why the things on your list are important to you.

5. WRITING

A. Write a description of one possession that is on the list you made in Exercise 4B. Explain why it is important to you. Here is what one student wrote.

> If I could save one possession, I would save the letters from my friends.
>
> Before I came to the United States, one of my friends wrote me this letter:
>
> "You will go to the United States soon. You may have many hard times before you adapt to your new environment. But don't forget that I am supporting you all the time. Even if I'm not close to you, I'll always be in your heart."
>
> Every time I feel homesick, I read his letter. It always cheers me up. How could I ever replace a possession like that?

Now write about a possession that you would save.

B. Every year thousands of tourists visit Pompeii. Have you ever been a tourist? Have you ever visited a beautiful or interesting place in your country or in another country? Write about it. Here is what one student wrote.

> ### My Visit to Kyoto, Japan
>
> I went to Kyoto in April this year. I stayed in a Japanese-style hotel. A mountain river ran past the hotel, and there was a wooden bridge over the river. From my hotel room I could see a mountain. The mountain was many colors of green, and at the foot of the mountain there were many cherry blossoms. The green colors and the cherry blossoms were reflected on the river. It was a beautiful view. My heart softened.

Now write your paragraph.

1. PRE-READING

Below are pairs of English words that sound alike. Your teacher will say one word from each pair. Circle the word that you hear.

1. feel   fill
2. they   day
3. men   man
4. ice   eyes
5. cap   cup
6. glass   grass
7. hot   hat
8. thought   taught
9. thick   sick
10. jello   yellow
11. fifteen   fifty
12. bomb   bum
13. Oakland   Auckland

After you finish this exercise, your teacher will tell you the correct answers. Was the exercise difficult for you? If it was, don't worry—it's difficult for native speakers of English, too. In this story you will learn how the last two pairs of words caused *big* problems for people whose native language is English.

Misunderstandings

HE had uncombed hair, dirty clothes, and only 35 cents in his pocket. In Baltimore, Maryland, he got on a bus and headed straight for the restroom. He thought that if he hid in the restroom, he could ride to New York without paying. But a passenger at the back of the bus saw him. She tapped the person in front of her on the shoulder and said, "There's a bum in the restroom. Tell the bus driver." That passenger tapped the person sitting in front of him. "Tell the bus driver there's a bum in the restroom," he said.

The message was passed from person to person until it reached the front of the bus. But somewhere along the way, the message changed. By the time it reached the bus driver, it was not "There's a *bum* in the restroom" but "There's a *bomb* in the restroom." The driver immediately pulled over to the side of the highway and radioed the police. When the police arrived, they told the passengers to get off the bus and stay far away. Then they closed the highway. That soon caused a 15-mile-long traffic jam. With the help of a dog, the police searched the bus for two hours. Of course, they found no bomb.

Two similar-sounding English words also caused trouble for a man who wanted to fly from Los Angeles to Oakland, California. His problems began at the airport in Los Angeles. He thought he heard his flight announced, so he walked to the gate, showed his ticket, and got on the plane. Twenty minutes after takeoff, the man began to worry. Oakland was north of Los Angeles, but the plane seemed to be heading west, and when he looked out his window all he could see was ocean. "Is this plane going to Oakland?" he asked the flight attendant. The flight attendant gasped. "No," she said. We're going to *Auckland*—Auckland, New Zealand."

Because so many English words sound similar, misunderstandings among English-speaking people are not uncommon. Not all misunderstandings result in highways being closed or passengers flying to the wrong continent. Most misunderstandings are much less serious. Every day people speaking English ask one another questions like these: "Did you say seven*ty* or seven*teen*?" "Did you say that you *can* come or that you *can't*?" Similar-sounding words can be especially confusing for people who speak English as a second language.

When a Korean woman who lives in the United States arrived at work one morning, her boss asked her, "Did you get a plate?" "No...," she answered, wondering what in the world he meant. She worked in an office. Why did the boss ask her about a plate? All day she wondered about her boss's strange question, but she was too embarrassed to ask him about it. At five o'clock, when she was getting ready to go home, her boss said, "Please be on time tomorrow. You were 15 minutes late this morning." "Sorry," she said. "My car wouldn't start, and...." Suddenly she stopped talking and began to smile. Now she understood. Her boss hadn't asked her, "Did you get a plate?" He had asked her, "Did you get up late?"

English is not the only language with similar-sounding words. Other languages, too, have words that can cause misunderstandings, especially for foreigners.

An English-speaking woman who was traveling in Mexico saw a sign in front of a restaurant. The sign said that the special that day was "*sopa con jamón y cebollas.*" She knew that was Spanish for "soup with ham and onions." That sounded good. As the woman walked to her table, she practiced ordering. She whispered to herself, "*Sopa con jamón y cebollas. Sopa con jamón y cebollas.*" Then she sat down, and a waiter came to take her order. "*Sopa con jabón y caballos,*" she said. "What?" the waiter asked. No wonder the waiter didn't understand. The woman had just ordered a very unusual lunch: soup with soap and horses.

Auckland and *Oakland*. "A plate" and "up late." *Jamón* and *jabón*. When similar-sounding words cause a misunderstanding, probably the best thing to do is just laugh and learn from the mistake. Of course, sometimes it's hard to laugh. The man who traveled to Auckland instead of Oakland didn't feel like laughing. But even that misunderstanding turned out all right in the end. The airline paid for the man's hotel room and meals in New Zealand and for his flight back to California. "Oh well," the man later said, "I always wanted to see New Zealand."

2. VOCABULARY

A. LOOKING AT THE STORY

Which words have the same meaning as the words in the story? Circle the letter of the correct answer.

1. She *tapped the person* in front of her *on the shoulder.*
   - **a.** touched the person's shoulder lightly with her hand
   - **b.** pushed hard on the person's shoulder

2. "There's a *bum* in the restroom."
   - **a.** person who doesn't work and probably doesn't have a home
   - **b.** person who travels by bus

3. The driver *pulled over* to the side of the highway.
   - **a.** looked
   - **b.** moved

4. The driver *radioed the police.*
   - **a.** called the police on his radio
   - **b.** got the attention of a police car

5. That soon caused a *15-mile-long traffic jam.*
   - **a.** line of stopped cars that was 15 miles long
   - **b.** line of cars going only 15 miles per hour

6. The police *searched the bus* for two hours.
   - **a.** looked everywhere on the bus
   - **b.** drove everywhere with the bus

7. Twenty minutes after *takeoff,* the man began to worry.
   - **a.** the plane went up into the air
   - **b.** the man took off his jacket

8. "Is this plane going to Oakland?" he asked the *flight attendant.*
   - **a.** person who flies an airplane
   - **b.** person who takes care of the passengers on an airplane

9. Misunderstandings among English-speaking people are *not uncommon.*
   - **a.** never happen
   - **b.** happen often

10. Not all misunderstandings *result in highways being closed.*
   - **a.** mean that highways are closed
   - **b.** cause highways to be closed

11. She *whispered* to herself, "Sopa con jamón y cebollas."
   - **a.** talked very quietly
   - **b.** thought very seriously

12. But even that misunderstanding *turned out all right in the end.*
   - **a.** was OK after the plane turned back
   - **b.** had a happy ending

B. LOOKING AT SPECIAL EXPRESSIONS

Find the best way to complete each sentence. Write the letter of your answer on the line.

to head straight for = to go immediately to

1. _____ He got on the bus and

2. _____ When the children arrived at the park,

3. _____ We were hungry, so when we got home,

      a. they headed straight for the playground.

      b. headed straight for the restroom.

      c. we headed straight for the kitchen.

by the time = when

4. _____ By the time it reached the bus driver,

5. _____ By the time I got home from the store,

6. _____ By the time we got to the theater,

      d. the message was "There's a bomb in the restroom."

      e. the best seats were taken.

      f. the ice cream had melted.

The expression "in the world" is used with a question word to show surprise.

7. _____ "No, I didn't get a plate," she answered, wondering

8. _____ When the phone rang at 1 A.M., he wondered

9. _____ When we told her we were going for a walk, she asked us

      g. why in the world we were going outside in such bad weather.

      h. who in the world would call at that hour.

      i. what in the world he meant.

no wonder = it's not surprising

10. _____ No wonder the waiter didn't understand;

11. _____ No wonder you're tired;

12. _____ No wonder you didn't do well on the test;

      j. you didn't go to bed until after midnight last night.

      k. the woman had just ordered a very unusual lunch.

      l. you didn't study.

to feel like = to want to

13. _____ The man who traveled to Auckland instead of Oakland

14. _____ Let's go to the party;

15. _____ I'll eat just a sandwich;

      m. didn't feel like laughing.

      n. I feel like dancing.

      o. I don't feel like eating a big dinner.

3. COMPREHENSION/READING SKILLS

A. UNDERSTANDING CAUSE AND EFFECT

Find the best way to complete each sentence. Write the letter of your answer on the line.

1. _____ The man hid in the restroom

2. _____ There was a 15-mile-long traffic jam

3. _____ The man who wanted to fly to Oakland was worried

4. _____ The Korean woman didn't ask her boss about his strange question

5. _____ Her boss asked her, "Did you get up late?"

a. because the police closed the highway.

b. because he didn't want to pay for his bus ride.

c. because she had arrived at work 15 minutes late.

d. because the plane seemed to be heading west, not north.

e. because she was too embarrassed.

B. UNDERSTANDING DETAILS

Read the sentences from the story. One word in each sentence is not correct. Find the word and cross it out. Write the correct word.

1. He had uncombed hair, dirty clothes, and only 35 dollars in his pocket.

2. In Baltimore, Maryland, he got on a train and headed straight for the restroom.

3. He thought that if he hid in the restroom, he could ride to Washington without paying.

4. But a driver in the back of the bus saw him.

5. She tapped the passenger in front of her on the foot and said, "There's a bum in the restroom."

Now copy three sentences from the story, but change one word in each sentence so that the information is not correct. Give your sentences to a classmate. Your classmate will find the incorrect word in each sentence, cross it out, and write the correct word. When your classmate is finished, check the corrections.

6. _____

_____

7. _____

_____

8. _____

_____

4. DISCUSSION

A. Think about these questions. Discuss your answers with your classmates.

1. In your country, if someone tried to ride a bus without paying, what do you think other passengers would do? What would you do?
2. Have you ever confused two similar-sounding English words? Which two words did you confuse? What happened?
3. In your native language, are there similar-sounding words (like *seventy* and *seventeen*) that people sometimes confuse? What are the words?

B. The message "There's a bum in the restroom" changed as people passed it to the front of the bus. Will a message that is passed around your classroom change, too? To find out, play the telephone game.

One of your classmates (Classmate #1) will whisper a message to a classmate sitting nearby (Classmate #2). The message can be anything, for example, "The weather in Thailand is warmer than the weather here" or "When are we going to have a coffee break?" Classmate #2 will whisper the message to Classmate #3. Classmate #3 will whisper the message to Classmate #4, and so on. (When a classmate whispers the message to you, you may *not* ask him or her to repeat it. You must pass the message you hear, even if it makes no sense.) The last classmate to hear the message will say it out loud. Is it the same message that Classmate #1 whispered?

5. WRITING

A. "I always wanted to see New Zealand," the man who flew to Auckland said. Is there a place that you've always wanted to see? Why do you want to go there? What sights do you want to see? Write about a place you've always wanted to visit.

B. The woman in the story ordered soup with soap and horses. Have you ever had a misunderstanding about food? Have you ever had a problem eating at someone's house, or buying food at a supermarket, or ordering food at a restaurant? Write about your experience. Here is what one student wrote.

On a visit to the United States, I went to a restaurant with my friends. I ordered a salad. The waitress asked me, "What kind of dressing do you want on your salad — blue cheese, ranch, Thousand Island, Italian, or French?" Of course, I said "French" because I am French. When the waitress brought the salad, I was shocked. The dressing was orange. I had never seen dressing like that in France. Then I tasted it. It tasted terrible. I never ordered "French" dressing again.

Now write about your experience.

---

1. PRE-READING

Look at the picture and think about these questions. Discuss your answers with your classmates.

- What is a thrift store?
- In your native country, do you have thrift stores or other places where you can buy things cheaply? Describe them to your classmates.
- The men in the picture are looking at something that one of the men bought at a thrift store. What do you think it is? Why do you think the man on the right looks so happy?

A Real Bargain

A FEW years ago Ed Jones was shopping at a thrift store in Indianapolis, Indiana. He walked past the used clothing and stopped at the used books. He looked at the books and then at some old dishes. Mr. Jones was looking for something that might be valuable. If he found something valuable, he would buy it cheaply and then resell it, perhaps to an antique dealer. But today Mr. Jones didn't see anything he wanted, so he started walking toward the door. Then something caught his eye. Leaning against a wall there was a large cardboard map.

Mr. Jones walked over for a closer look. The map was covered with dust, so Mr. Jones wiped it with his handkerchief. Under the dust was a color map of Paris. It looked old. On the back of the map, someone had written the price: $3. Mr. Jones was quite certain that the map was worth more than three dollars, so he bought it. He thought he could probably sell it for $40.

Later, at home, Mr. Jones looked more closely at the map. He decided it might be very old. Maybe it was worth even more than $40.

The next day Mr. Jones took the map to a geography professor at a nearby university. The professor was a map expert. After looking at the map for a few minutes, he became very excited. "I've read about this map!" he exclaimed. Then he told Mr. Jones what he knew.

In 1671 the king of France, Louis XIV, asked a cartographer to make a map of Paris. The cartographer worked on the map for four years. The map he drew was beautiful—it was not just a map, but a work of art as well. The cartographer made several black and white copies of the map. Then he carefully colored one of the copies, using blue for rivers, green for trees, and brown for buildings. The professor said that one black and white copy of the map was in the British Museum in London, and another was in the Bibliotheque Nationale in Paris. "I think," the professor told Mr. Jones, "that you've just found the color copy of the map—in a thrift store in Indianapolis!" The professor suggested that Mr. Jones take the map to New York City. Experts there could tell Mr. Jones if the professor was right.

The New York experts said the professor *was* right. They told Mr. Jones that he had the only color copy of the map and that it was extremely valuable. "How much do you think it's worth?" Mr. Jones asked the experts. "Millions," they replied. "It's impossible to say exactly how much the map is worth. It's worth whatever someone is willing to pay for it."

Soon Mr. Jones discovered how much people were willing to pay for the map. Someone offered him 10 million dollars; then someone else immediately offered him 12 million. The most recent offer was 19.5 million dollars. Mr. Jones hasn't decided whether he will sell his three-dollar map at that price or wait for a higher offer. He is thinking it over.

But how in the world did this map find its way to a thrift store in Indianapolis? Here is what some experts think: The map was probably in a museum or in the home of a wealthy family in France. Then a thief stole it, perhaps during the confusion of World War I or World War II. The thief sold the map to an antique dealer in France. The French antique dealer, not knowing how valuable the map was, sold it to an antique dealer in Indianapolis. That antique dealer, who also did not know its value, gave it to a neighbor. For ten years the map hung on a wall in the neighbor's house. Then the neighbor got tired of it and sold it to the thrift store. The map sat in the thrift store for months. Finally Mr. Jones discovered it.

When Mr. Jones went shopping at the thrift store, he was looking for a bargain. He wanted to find something that was worth more than the price he paid. He paid three dollars for the map, and it is worth at least 19.5 million dollars. Now *that's* a bargain!

2. VOCABULARY

A. LOOKING AT THE STORY

Which words have the same meaning as the words in the story? Circle the letter of the correct answer.

1. Ed Jones was shopping at a *thrift store.*
   a. store that sells used things at low prices
   b. store that sells expensive things at high prices

2. If he found something valuable, he could resell it, perhaps to an *antique dealer.*
   a. a person who fixes broken things
   b. a person who buys and sells old things

3. Leaning against a wall of the store there was a large *cardboard* map.
   a. made of heavy paper
   b. made of plastic

4. Mr. Jones was quite *certain* that the map was worth more than three dollars.
   a. worried
   b. sure

5. The next day Mr. Jones took the map to a *geography* professor at a nearby university.
   a. the study of the world's countries, cities, oceans, rivers, and mountains
   b. the study of the world's history, languages, and customs

6. "I've read about this map!" he *exclaimed.*
   a. said with strong feeling
   b. said very quietly

7. Louis XIV asked a *cartographer* to make a map of Paris.
   a. a person who draws maps
   b. a person who writes books

8. The New York experts told Mr. Jones that his map was *extremely* valuable.
   a. not really
   b. very

9. "How much do you think it's worth?" Mr. Jones asked the experts. "Millions," they *replied.*
   a. answered
   b. asked

10. Someone *offered him ten million dollars.*
    a. said, "Will you take ten million dollars for the map?"
    b. told him, "I think your map is worth ten million dollars."

11. Some experts think the map was probably in a museum or in the home of a *wealthy* family in France.
    a. famous
    b. rich

12. When Mr. Jones went shopping at the thrift store, he was looking for a *bargain.*
    a. something that can be bought cheaply
    b. something that has been used

B. LOOKING AT SPECIAL EXPRESSIONS

Find the best way to complete each sentence on p. 47. Write the letter of your answer on the line.

to catch one's eye = to get one's attention

1. _____ Mr. Jones was walking toward the door

2. _____ She was leaving the museum

3. _____ He was walking through the department store

a. when a painting by Renoir caught her eye.

b. when a large cardboard map caught his eye.

c. when a sweater caught his eye.

to be worth = to have a value of

4. _____ Mr. Jones was quite certain that

5. _____ They paid $80,000 for their house, but

6. _____ He tried to sell his old TV for $500, but nobody bought it because

d. the map was worth more than three dollars.

e. it wasn't worth more than $250.

f. it was worth at least $100,000.

to be willing to = to be ready to

7. _____ The map was worth whatever

8. _____ Our teacher said that

9. _____ I won't have to take the bus because my friend said

g. he was willing to give us extra help after class.

h. she was willing to drive me to the airport.

i. someone was willing to pay for it.

to get tired of = to become no longer interested in

10. _____ The neighbor got tired of the map and

11. _____ He got tired of hamburgers

12. _____ I'm getting tired of studying French;

j. after eating them every day for a month.

k. sold it to a thrift store.

l. maybe I'll study Spanish next year.

3. COMPREHENSION/READING SKILLS

A. UNDERSTANDING CAUSE AND EFFECT

Find the best way to complete each sentence. Write the letter of your answer on the line.

1. _____ Ed Jones went to the thrift store

2. _____ He wiped the map with his handkerchief

3. _____ The professor suggested that Mr. Jones take the map to New York City

4. _____ Experts in New York said the map was extremely valuable

5. _____ The map was a bargain

a. because experts there could tell Mr. Jones if the professor was right.

b. because it was cheap but very valuable.

c. because he was looking for a bargain.

d. because it was the only color copy.

e. because it was covered with dust.

B. UNDERSTANDING DETAILS

Read the sentences from the story. One word in each sentence is not correct. Find the word and cross it out. Write the correct word.

1. The map was covered with paint.

2. Under the dust Mr. Jones found a color map of Rome.

3. The map looked new.

4. On the back of the map, someone had written the price: $30.

5. The next day Mr. Jones took the map to a mathematics professor at the university.

Now copy three sentences from the story, but change one word in each sentence so that the information is not correct. Give your sentences to a classmate. Your classmate will find the incorrect word in each sentence, cross it out, and write the correct word. When your classmate is finished, check the corrections.

6. _____

_____

7. _____

_____

8. _____

_____

4. DISCUSSION

A. Think about these questions. Discuss your answers with your classmates.

1. After reading the story, do you think you might go to a thrift store to look for something valuable?

2. Have you—or has anyone you know—ever had an experience similar to Mr. Jones's experience? Have you ever bought something at a low price and then discovered it was worth more than you paid for it? Have you ever had the opposite experience? Have you ever bought something at a high price and then discovered that it was worth less than you paid for it?

B. Be a cartographer. Draw a map of a country you know. Put important rivers, mountains, cities, and tourist attractions on the map. Then show your map to a classmate. Tell your classmate about the places on your map.

5. WRITING

A. What would you do if, like Mr. Jones, you suddenly had 19.5 million dollars? How would you use the money? Make a list of what you would do.

1. _____
   _____

2. _____
   _____

3. _____
   _____

4. _____
   _____

5. _____

B. Imagine that you went to a thrift store and bought something cheaply. The object could be jewelry, a book, a painting, a photograph, a toy, a vase—or anything else that you want it to be. Imagine that later you discovered that the object you bought is very valuable—that it's worth much, much more than you paid for it.

Make up a story. In the story, describe what you bought, tell what it's really worth, and explain why it's valuable. Here is what one student wrote.

I bought a dress at a thrift store. It was red and made of lace. It was only one dollar.

I wore the dress to a party. A woman at the party stared at me for a long time. Then she asked me, "Where did you get that dress?" "I got it from a friend," I answered. That was not true, but I didn't want to say that I had bought it at a thrift store for only one dollar. "That was Miss K's dress," the woman said. "She wore it at her last concert." (Miss K was a famous singer.) "I'm a great fan of Miss K's," the woman continued. "I have all her cassettes, and I have many photographs of her. But I don't have anything that she wore. Will you please sell me that dress? I don't know what your friend paid for it, but I'm willing to pay $500."

I told her she could have the dress for $500 and went home from the party very happy.

Now write about the object that you bought.

1. PRE-READING

Are you superstitious? Read the sentences. Then check "yes" or "no."

	Yes	No
1. Black cats are unlucky.	——	——
2. It is unlucky to break a mirror.	——	——
3. If I point at the moon, something bad will happen to me.	——	——
4. It is bad luck when a shoelace breaks.	——	——
5. If my palm itches, I will receive money.	——	——
6. When I want good luck, I sometimes cross my fingers or knock on wood.	——	——
7. I have a lucky number.	——	——
8. I have something that I consider lucky—a lucky pen or a lucky hat, for example.	——	——

If you checked "yes" after any of these statements, you are probably a little superstitious.

Who in your class is superstitious?
Who in your class is not superstitious?

Black Cats and Broken Mirrors

DO you think that it is bad luck to walk under a ladder or break a mirror? Do you think that black cats and the number 13 are unlucky? The three men in the picture don't. Every Friday the 13th they walk under ladders, break mirrors, and open umbrellas indoors. They want to prove that they aren't at all superstitious. They may be the only people in the world who aren't. There are over one million superstitions, and most people believe at least one or two of them.

Many people are superstitious about numbers. They think that there are lucky numbers and unlucky numbers. The number 13 is often considered unlucky. In some parts of the world, buildings have no 13th floor and streets have no houses with the number 13. In Japan, 4 is considered unlucky because in Japanese the word "four" is pronounced the same as the word "death." Japanese never give gifts of four knives, four napkins, or four of anything. What are the lucky numbers? Seven is a lucky number in many places, and 8 is considered lucky in Japan and China. In China, businesses often open on August 8 (8-8), and many couples register to get married at eight past eight on August 8.

Superstitions about numbers are so widespread that some people—called numerologists—make a living giving advice about numbers. In 1937, when the Toyoda family of Japan wanted to form a car company, they asked a numerologist if "Toyoda" would be a good name for the company. The numerologist said it would not be. He explained that "Toyoda" took ten strokes of the pen to write, and 10 was not a lucky number. "Toyota," however, took eight strokes to write, and eight was a very lucky number. The numerologist recommended "Toyota" as a better name for the company. The family took his advice. As a result, millions of people drive "Toyotas" and not "Toyodas."

In addition to superstitions about numbers, there are many other kinds of superstitions. There are superstitions about eating, sleeping, sneezing, and itching. There are superstitions about animals and holidays and horseshoes. There are even superstitions about superstitions. Those superstitions tell people how to reverse bad luck.

For example, in many parts of the world spilling salt is bad luck. Throwing salt, however, is good luck. So, people who spill salt throw a little of the spilled salt over their left shoulder. Throwing the spilled salt reverses the bad luck. When the Japanese bump heads, they immediately bump heads again. According to a Japanese superstition, the first bump means their parents will die, but the second bump "erases" the first bump. To reverse bad luck in general, people turn around three times, turn their pockets inside out, or put their hats on backwards. In the United States, baseball players sometimes wear their caps backwards when their team is losing. It looks silly, but the baseball players don't mind if it helps them win the game.

Because there are so many superstitions, it is not surprising that some of them are contradictory. In Germany, it is good luck when the left eye twitches and bad luck when the right eye twitches. In Malaysia, it is exactly the opposite: a twitching right eye means good luck, and a twitching left eye means bad luck. Accidentally putting on clothes inside out brings good luck in Pakistan but bad luck in Costa Rica. In Chile, unmarried people won't take the last piece of food on the plate because it means they will never marry. In Thailand, unmarried people take the last piece because it means they will marry someone good-looking.

Some superstitions have been with us for so long that they have become customs. In many parts of the world it is polite to say "Health" or "God bless you" when someone sneezes. People used to think that the soul could escape from the body during a sneeze. They said "God bless you" to protect people from losing their souls. Today we no longer believe that people who sneeze are in danger of losing their souls, but we say "God bless you" anyway. We say it not because we are superstitious, but because we are polite.

Even people who say they aren't superstitious would probably not do what the men in the picture do—intentionally walk under ladders and break mirrors. Almost everyone is at least a little superstitious. One woman says that when she got married, her aunt gave her white bath towels. "Never buy purple towels," her aunt said. "If you use purple towels, your marriage will end." Does the woman believe that superstition? "No, of course not," she says. "It's silly." Does she use purple towels? "Well, no," she answers. "Why take chances?"

2. VOCABULARY

A. LOOKING AT THE STORY

Which words or picture has the same meaning as the words in the reading selection? Circle the letter of the correct answer.

1. Do you think that it is bad luck to walk under a *ladder*?

   a. (In the photo on page 50, the man on the right is standing under it.)   **b.** (In the photo on page 50, the man in the center is standing under it.)

2. The men walk under ladders and break mirrors to *prove* that they aren't superstitious.

   a. believe it is crazy   **b.** show it is true

3. Superstitions about numbers are *widespread*.

   a. found in many places   **b.** believed only by children

4. Some people *make a living* giving people advice about numbers.

   a. make money   **b.** make mistakes

5. "Toyota" took *eight strokes* of the pen to write.

   a.    **b.**

6. The family *took his advice*.

   a. did what he suggested   **b.** asked for more information

7. There are superstitions that *reverse bad luck*.

   a. change bad luck to good luck   **b.** give the bad luck to someone else

8. If you *spill salt*, immediately throw a little of the spilled salt over your left shoulder.

   a. use too much salt   **b.** pour out salt accidentally

9. It looks silly, but *the baseball players don't mind* if it helps them win the game.

   a. that's OK with the baseball players   **b.** the baseball players don't like to think about it

10. Some superstitions *are contradictory*. In Germany, it is good luck when the left eye twitches. In Malaysia, it is bad luck when the left eye twitches.

    a. are very old   **b.** mean the opposite

11. Putting clothes on *inside out* brings good luck in Pakistan.

    a. in the house, rather than outside   **b.** with the inside parts on the outside

12. People used to think that the soul could *escape from* the body during a sneeze.

    a. enter   **b.** leave

B. LOOKING AT SPECIAL EXPRESSIONS

Find the best way to complete each sentence. Write the letter of your answer on the line.

as a result = because of that

1. _____ The family took the numerologist's advice. As a result,

2. _____ He overslept. As a result,

3. _____ She didn't study; as a result,

a. he was late for work.

b. she didn't do well on the test.

c. millions of people today drive "Toyotas" and not "Toyodas."

in addition to = as well as ("In addition to" connects two similar ideas.)

4. _____ In addition to the superstitions about numbers,

5. _____ In addition to studying French,

6. _____ In addition to being an excellent student

d. she is an excellent dancer and swimmer.

e. there are many other kinds of superstitions.

f. he is studying German and Spanish.

according to Mr. Jones = Mr. Jones says that

7. _____ According to a Japanese superstition,

8. _____ According to my watch,

9. _____ According to this map,

g. the museum is on Michigan Avenue.

h. the first bump means your parents will die.

i. it's a quarter to nine.

3. COMPREHENSION/READING SKILLS

A. UNDERSTANDING THE MAIN IDEAS

What information is *not* in the story? Draw a line through the three sentences with information that is not in the story.

• The men in the picture want to prove they are not superstitious.
• There are over one million superstitions.
• Children are usually not superstitious.
• Many people are superstitious about numbers.
• Numerologists make a living giving people advice about numbers.
• It is always a good idea to take a numerologist's advice.
• Some superstitions tell people how to reverse bad luck.
• Some superstitions are contradictory.
• Some superstitions have become customs.
• People who use purple towels are silly.
• Almost everyone is at least a little superstitious.

B. UNDERSTANDING SUPPORTING DETAILS

Find the best way to complete each sentence. Write the letter of your answer on the line.

1. _____ Many people are superstitious about numbers. For example,

2. _____ Some people—called numerologists—make a living giving people advice about numbers. For example,

3. _____ There are superstitions that tell people how to reverse bad luck. For example,

4. _____ Some superstitions are contradictory. For example,

5. _____ Some superstitions have been with us for so long that they have become customs. For example,

a. accidentally putting on clothes inside out brings good luck in Pakistan but bad luck in Costa Rica.

b. it is polite to say "Health" or "God bless you" when someone sneezes.

c. throwing spilled salt over the left shoulder reverses bad luck.

d. the number 13 is often considered unlucky.

e. a numerologist recommended "Toyota" as a name for the car company.

4. DISCUSSION

Form small conversation groups. Ask the people in your group if they know any superstitions about:

salt	rabbits	eye twitching	sleeping
ladders	elephants	shivering	dreams
mirrors	horseshoes	whistling	leaving the house
brooms	garlic	cutting nails	finding a coin
combs	four-leaf clovers	taking photos	opening an umbrella
knives	numbers	giving gifts	knocking on wood
shoes	hiccups	cooking	weddings
black cats	itching	eating a pear	New Year's Day
crows	sneezing	dropping silverware	funeral processions
owls	ears ringing	chopsticks	

5. WRITING

A. Make a list of superstitions that some people in your country believe. Here is an example from a student from Panama:

1. Always sleep with your feet facing the door of your room.
2. If you give your sweetheart a handkerchief or socks, you will argue.
3. If you want a visitor to leave, turn your broom upside down.
4. If a young woman is sweeping the floor and the broom accidentally touches her feet, she will marry a rich old man.
5. To protect yourself from evil spirits, wear your pajamas inside out.

Now make your list.

B. Write about something you have that is lucky—a lucky number or a lucky hat, for example. Why is it lucky? Can you remember a time when it brought you good luck? Here is what one student wrote.

When I was a high school student, I had a difficult mathematics test one day. Before the test our teacher told us, "Use the same pencil you used when you studied last night. When you can't solve a problem, hold the pencil tightly. If you do that, you will be able to solve the problem." I did that, and I got every answer right. I thought, "This is my lucky pencil." But later I discovered that my pencil was lucky only sometimes. When I studied hard, my pencil helped me, but when I didn't study hard, it didn't help me.

Now write about something you have that is lucky.

C. Has there ever been a time when you've had very good—or very bad—luck? Write about it. Here is what one student wrote.

Last month I had a very unlucky day. I overslept in the morning because I had forgotten to set my alarm clock. It was raining. On the way to the bus stop I fell and got wet. Then I missed the bus and was late for my class.

That night a friend of mine called me while I was cooking dinner. It was a long phone call, and I forgot about my dinner. When I finished talking to my friend, I went into the kitchen to check on my dinner. It was burned. I thought, "I have only two hands and one head. I'm trying to do too much." But later I thought, "I was just not lucky today."

Now write about a time when you had good luck or bad luck.

1. PRE-READING

Which of these statements do you think is true? Check one.

1. _____ Women work harder than men.

2. _____ Men work harder than women.

3. _____ Both men and women work hard.

Now, as a class, answer these questions.

- How many people in the class checked #1? How many checked #2? How many checked #3?
- Why did you check the statement you did? Were you thinking about your own family? Were you thinking about men and women everywhere, or only in your native country?
- Did people from the same country check the same statement? Did the men in the class check the same statement? Did the women in the class check the same statement?

Mother's Camp

THE women in the picture have everything they need for a wonderful vacation. They have beautiful scenery and warm, sunny weather. They have hotel rooms that are just a few minutes' walk from a clear blue lake. They have time for swimming, boating, and hiking. What they *don't* have are their husbands and children—and that, they say, is what makes their vacation *really* wonderful. The women left their husbands and children at home and are spending a weekend at a resort called Mother's Camp. At Mother's Camp, husbands and children are not allowed.

Why would a woman want to take a vacation without her family? Some mothers say they need time to be alone. "At home the only place where I can be by myself is the bathroom," one woman said. At Mother's Camp a woman has a room to herself. She can sleep, read, or watch TV, and no one will bother her. No children will ask, "Mom, what's for dinner?" No husband will say, "Honey, I can't find any clean socks."

Other women go to Mother's Camp not to be alone, but to be with women who are in similar situations. "I work full-time and have two kids," one woman says. "I take care of my husband, too. I'm incredibly busy. At Mother's Camp I meet other women who are working and raising families. We talk and talk. It helps me to know that other women have the same problems I do."

Actually, *many* women have the same problems she does. Almost 50 percent of women in the United States work outside the home. Many of them work full-time and then come home to a second job—taking care of their homes and families. These working women say one of their biggest problems is housework.

In the United States, working wives do about 75 percent of the housework. Many of their husbands say they want to help. But then they burn the rice or they can't find the pans. They ask so many questions that their wives decide it is easier to do the job themselves. Also, many husbands don't do daily jobs, like making dinner or washing dishes. They do jobs they can do when they have some free time, like washing clothes or fixing things that are broken. Many wives think that their husbands need to do more of the daily housework; many husbands admit that they aren't doing enough.

Some women go to Mother's Camp just to get a break from housework. For two days they don't cook, they don't clean, and they don't do laundry. What do they do? They relax in the sun, go for boat rides, and sing songs around the campfire. In the evening, they get massages and sip champagne. Mostly, they try to escape, at least for one weekend, the responsibilities of being a wife and mother.

Recently a woman who was staying at Mother's Camp decided to spend an entire afternoon lying on the beach. She took a towel, her sunglasses, and a book, and she headed for the door of the hotel. Just as she was walking out the door, she heard the telephone ring. She turned around, laughing, and said, "If that's my husband or kids, tell them you haven't seen me!" Of course, she was just kidding . . . wasn't she?

2. VOCABULARY

A. LOOKING AT THE STORY

Sue, a working mother, spent a weekend at Mother's Camp. While she was there, she wrote a letter to her friend Maria. Some words are missing from Sue's letter. Write the correct word(s) on the line.

scenery	resort	bothers	raising a family	admits	responsibilities
hiking	allowed	situation	a break	sip	entire

Saturday, 9 P.M.

Dear Maria,

I am spending the weekend at a _____ called "Mother's Camp." Jim
                                                    1
and the kids aren't with me because husbands and children aren't _____
                                                                        2
here.

I spent the day in my room, just reading and watching TV. It was wonderful! My kids
didn't say, "Mom, I need help!" and my husband didn't ask me, "Honey, what's for
dinner?" Nobody _____ me here.
                         3

At dinner I met a woman named Regina, who has two children. She's doing what I'm
doing—working full-time and _____ . Her _____ is very
                                      4   5
similar to mine.

After dinner Regina and I sat at the table and talked. We were happy we didn't have to
wash the dishes. It's so good to get _____ from housework. At our house
                                            6
I do almost all of the housework. Jim _____ that he isn't doing enough.
                                             7

Tomorrow morning I'm going to put on my walking shoes and do some
_____ . There are mountains and a lake here, so I want to get out and
        8
see the _____ . Then I'm going to spend from 1 o'clock to 5 o'clock—the
              9
_____ afternoon—swimming and boating. In the evening I'll just sit
      10
around the campfire and _____ champagne.
                               11

It's nice to escape, at least for one weekend, the _____ of being a wife
                                                          12
and mother. Here I don't have to take care of my husband and kids, and I don't have to do
housework.

Love,
Sue

B. LOOKING AT A NEW CONTEXT

Read the sentences. Then write the correct word on the line.

bothers   allowed   sip

1. In some restaurants there are "no smoking" sections. Smoking is not _____ there.

2. Sometimes my neighbors have loud parties at night. The noise _____ me, and I can't sleep.

3. When my coffee is hot, I don't drink it fast. I _____ it.

Now make your own examples for these words:

scenery	resort	bother	raise a family	admit	responsibilities
hiking	allowed	situation	a break	sip	entire

First, form small groups. One student in each group is the "teacher." The "teacher" will write each word on a separate small piece of paper, fold the papers, and give one to each person in the group. The "teacher" will take a word, too. Hold your paper so that no one can see your word. Make up a little story for your word like the ones above. (Be careful not to say your word.) Your classmates will listen to your story and try to guess which word you have. Then listen to your classmates' stories and try to guess which words they have.

3. COMPREHENSION/READING SKILLS

A. UNDERSTANDING THE MAIN IDEAS

Circle the letter of the best answer.

1. Mother's Camp is a resort where
   a. the weather is always beautiful.
   b. men and children are not allowed.
   c. there are no single rooms.

2. Women go to Mother's Camp to
   a. be alone, talk to women who are in similar situations, or just get a break from housework.
   b. learn better ways of doing daily jobs like making dinner and washing dishes.
   c. swim, hike, go boating, and just relax with their families.

3. Women who work full-time and have families say one of their biggest problems is
   a. their bosses.
   b. housework.
   c. getting to work on time.

4. In the United States, working wives
   a. sleep only six hours a night.
   b. do one hour of housework every day.
   c. do about 75 percent of the housework.

5. Women at Mother's Camp don't
   a. swim, hike, or relax in the sun.
   b. get massages or sip champagne.
   c. cook, clean, or do laundry.

B. UNDERSTANDING SUPPORTING DETAILS

Find the best way to complete each sentence. Write the letter of your answer on the line.

1. _____ The women at Mother's Camp have everything they need for a wonderful vacation. For example,

   a. they don't wash dishes.

2. _____ No one will bother a mother at Mother's Camp. For example,

   b. no children will ask, "Mom, what's for dinner?"

3. _____ Many husbands don't do daily jobs. For example,

   c. they fix things that are broken.

4. _____ Many husbands do jobs that they can do when they have some free time. For example,

   d. they have beautiful scenery.

4. DISCUSSION

First complete the chart yourself. Read each question and check "yes" or "no." Then ask a classmate the questions. After your classmate answers "yes" or "no," ask "Why?" or "Why not?"

	YOU		YOUR CLASSMATE	
	Yes	No	Yes	No
1. Would you, or your wife, or your mother, like to go to Mother's Camp?				
2. If there were a Mother's Camp in your native country, do you think a lot of women would go there?				
3. Do you think Mother's Camp is a good idea?				
4. Do you think fathers need a Father's Camp—a resort where wives and children are not allowed?				
5. Do you think it is OK for mothers to work outside the home?				
6. If a married woman works full-time, do you think her husband should help with the housework?				

Now work as a class and answer the questions.

1. Are there any mothers in the class? Would they like to go to Mother's Camp? Why or why not?
2. In which countries would a Mother's Camp be popular? In which countries would it not be popular?
3. Is Mother's Camp a good idea? What did the women in the class answer? What did the men answer?
4. Are there any fathers in the class? Would they like to go to a Father's Camp? Why or why not?
5. Do you know any husbands who help with the housework? What jobs do they do?

5. WRITING

A. Look at the chart in the discussion exercise. Answer one of the questions in writing. Explain why you answered the way you did.

B. For some women, a weekend at Mother's Camp is a "dream vacation." What would your "dream vacation" be? Where would you go? How long would you stay there? What would you do? Here is what one student wrote.

> For my dream vacation I would go to Los Angeles, California. I would stay in one of the best hotels by the beach. I would stay there for a month. I would do exercises to keep in shape and go out with California girls.
>
> Every day I would go to the beach with my friends. We would play volleyball and then swim in the ocean. At night we would go to the best restaurants and then after dinner we would go to parties. It would be great.

Now write about your "dream vacation."

UNIT **11**

1. PRE-READING

Look at the pictures and answer the questions. Discuss your answers with your classmates.

■ The small island in the picture is off the coast of eastern Canada. There is a deep hole on the island. Men began digging in the hole in 1795—and men are still digging today. What do you think they are trying to find?

■ Digging in the hole is difficult. It is also dangerous: six men have died in the hole. Look at the drawing of the hole. Can you see why digging in the hole is difficult? Can you see why it is dangerous?

The Treasure Hunt

ON a summer afternoon in 1795 a teenage boy named Daniel McGinnis was exploring a tiny island off the eastern coast of Canada. He was walking through a meadow of tall grass when he noticed something strange. In the center of the meadow stood a huge oak tree with part of one branch cut off. The ground beneath that branch was lower than the surrounding ground. Daniel knew that pirates had once sailed in the waters around the island. Was this, he wondered, where they had buried their treasure?

The next day Daniel returned to the island with shovels and two friends. The boys began digging. Two feet down they discovered a layer of stones. Under the stones was a hole about 13 feet wide. It was filled with loose dirt. The boys kept digging for several days. Ten feet below the ground their shovels hit an oak floor. They broke through the floor and kept digging. Twenty feet below the ground they found another oak floor. They broke through it, too, and kept digging. But when they discovered another oak floor 30 feet below the ground, they decided that they couldn't dig any deeper. They gave up the search and left the island.

Eight years later Daniel McGinnis, now a young man, returned with a group of men to continue digging beneath the oak tree. Day after day the men dug in the hole. One evening, 98 feet below the ground, their shovels hit a large wooden box. The box had to be a treasure chest! Certain that the treasure was almost theirs, the men went home to rest until daylight. When they returned in the morning, there was an unpleasant surprise: the hole had nearly filled with water. The men couldn't remove the water. Once again, Daniel McGinnis had to give up the search.

Over the years, other search groups came to the island. They all had the same problem: the hole filled with water. Not until 1850 did someone discover why.

In 1850 a man from a search group was eating his lunch on a beach not far from the hole. The man noticed water bubbling up through the sand. He went and got other men from the search group. When they saw the water coming up through the sand, they, too, thought it was odd. The men decided to dig on the beach. What they found amazed them. Under the sand there were entrances to five tunnels. All five tunnels led to the hole.

Later search groups discovered more tunnels leading from another beach to the hole. Engineers examined the tunnels. They estimated that 20 people worked two years to build them. The tunnels were cleverly planned. If anyone digging in the hole dug deeper than 95 feet, ocean water came through the tunnels and filled the hole.

Although the water problem made digging almost impossible, more and more men came to dig on the island. The tunnels convinced them that the hole held a great treasure. None of the men found the treasure, however, and six men died trying.

In 1967 a group of investors put their money into a search for the treasure. They brought huge drills, pumps, and other machines to the island. After drilling 212 feet into the hole, workers sent down a video camera. The camera took pictures of three wooden chests and a human hand. But then the walls of the hole collapsed, nearly killing a worker who was in it. The investors decided that the search was too dangerous and gave it up. Then, in 1989, they decided to try again. They raised 10 million dollars for another search. They said that this time they would not stop digging until they found the treasure.

But is there a pirates' treasure at the bottom of the hole? A lot of people think so. A brown, stringy material covered the oak floors that search groups found every ten feet in the hole. That brown material came from coconut trees. Coconut trees do not grow in Canada; the nearest coconut trees are over 800 miles away. Pirate ships could have brought the coconuts to Canada. Also, a heart-shaped stone was found in the hole. It is very similar to one that was found with pirates' treasure in the Caribbean.

If there is a pirates' treasure, it won't be easy to find. There is still the problem of water filling the hole. And there is another problem. During the past 200 years, dozens of search groups have dug in the hole, and each search group made the hole bigger. The hole that was once 13 feet wide is now enormous. The oak tree is gone. Where is the hole that Daniel McGinnis found? Today nobody knows for sure, so it is impossible to know exactly where to dig.

The investors who paid 10 million dollars think they will find the treasure in spite of the problems. And they think that when they find it, they will get every penny of their money back, and much more. One investor says, "This could be one of the greatest treasures ever found." It could be. Or it could be a 10-million-dollar hole.

2. VOCABULARY

A. LOOKING AT THE STORY

Think about the story. Answer the questions.

1. Do *pirates* rob ships or banks?

   _____

2. Is *treasure* gold, silver, and jewels, or is it plates, glasses, and cups?

   _____

3. Are *shovels* used for digging or for seeing in the dark?

   _____

4. Is *oak* a type of grass or a type of wood?

   _____

5. When people are *amazed*, are they angry or surprised?

   _____

6. Did the engineers who *examined* the tunnels look quickly or look carefully?

   _____

7. The tunnels *convinced* people that the hole held great treasure. Did the tunnels make people feel sure that the hole held treasure, or did the tunnels make people not feel sure?

   _____

8. Do *investors* want to use money to make money or do they want to use money to help people?

   _____

9. Are *drills* machines that make roads or machines that make holes?

   _____

10. Why did the investors bring *pumps* to the island—to take water out of the hole, or to take pictures of the hole?

    _____

11. The investors *raised* 10 million dollars. Does this mean that they spent the money or collected the money?

    _____

12. Is an *enormous* hole big or small?

    _____

B. LOOKING AT SPECIAL EXPRESSIONS

Find the best way to complete each sentence. Write the letter of your answer on the line.

to give up = to stop working at; to stop trying

1. _____ The boys decided that they couldn't dig any deeper and

2. _____ I used to run a mile a day,

3. _____ He tried to call his mother yesterday, but the line was busy;

a. but I hurt my leg and had to give up running.

b. gave up their search.

c. he dialed her number for twenty minutes and then gave up.

3. COMPREHENSION/READING SKILLS

A. UNDERSTANDING TIME RELATIONSHIPS

What information is *not* correct? Draw a line through it.

1. Before 1795
   a. a deep hole was dug on an island.
   b. tunnels were built from beaches to the hole.
   c. the walls of the hole collapsed.
   d. pirates sailed in the waters off the eastern coast of Canada.

2. In 1795
   a. Daniel McGinnis discovered an oak tree with part of one branch cut off.
   b. Daniel McGinnis and two friends dug under the oak tree.
   c. investors raised lots of money to search for the treasure.
   d. oak floors were found, ten, twenty, and thirty feet below the ground.

3. Eight years after Daniel McGinnis discovered the hole,
   a. he returned with a group of men to continue digging.
   b. men digging 98 feet down hit a wooden object with their shovels.
   c. the hole filled with water.
   d. six men died trying to find the treasure.

4. In 1850
   a. a man from a search group ate his lunch on a beach not far from the hole.
   b. investors brought huge drills, pumps, and other machines to the island.
   c. a search group saw water coming up through the sand.
   d. men found tunnels that led from a beach to the hole.

5. In 1967
   a. a group of investors decided to put their money into a search for the treasure.
   b. workers drilled 212 feet and then sent down a video camera.
   c. workers discovered a layer of stones in the hole.
   d. the walls of the hole collapsed, nearly killing a worker who was in it.

B. SCANNING FOR INFORMATION

The underlined information is not correct. Find the correct information in the story and write it. Work quickly; try to complete this exercise in three minutes or less.

1. In 1795 a teenage boy named Daniel <u>McDonald</u> was exploring a tiny island off the eastern coast of Canada.

2. In the center of the meadow stood a huge <u>maple</u> tree with part of one branch cut off.

3. <u>Two days later</u> Daniel returned to the island with shovels and two friends.

4. <u>Three</u> feet down they discovered a layer of stones.

5. Under the stones was a hole about <u>12</u> feet wide.

6. <u>Ten</u> years later Daniel McGinnis, now a young man, returned with a group of men to continue digging beneath the oak tree.

7. One <u>afternoon</u>, 98 feet below the ground, their shovels hit a large wooden box.

8. In <u>1860</u> a man from a search group was eating his lunch on a beach not far from the hole.

9. Under the sand the man found entrances to <u>four</u> tunnels.

10. Engineers estimate that <u>40</u> people worked two years to build them.

4. DISCUSSION

A. Talk about the hole. First answer the questions by checking "yes" or "no."

	YES	NO
1. The hole, with its oak floors and water tunnels, is complicated. Many people say that no group of pirates could have dug the hole. What do you think? Did pirates dig the hole?		
2. Do you think that there is a great treasure in the hole?		
3. If you had $10,000, would you invest your money in a search for the treasure?		
4. Would you like to go to the island and dig for the treasure?		

Now work as a class and answer these questions.

1. How many students think that pirates dug the hole? (If the pirates didn't dig the hole, then who did?)
2. How many students think there is a great treasure in the hole? What do they think the treasure is? How much do they think it's worth? (One investor says, "Billions of dollars." Is that possible?)
3. How many students would invest $10,000 in a search for the treasure?
4. How many students would like to go to the island and dig for the treasure? Why do those students want to go there? Why do some students *not* want to go there?

B. Talk about other treasures. Think about these questions and discuss your answers with your classmates.

1. Has a great treasure ever been discovered in your native country? What was the treasure? Who buried it? Who discovered it? What happened to it?
2. Do you know about any other searches for treasure? What were the searchers looking for? What did they find?

5. WRITING

One of the investors says, "This could be one of the greatest treasures ever found." What is your greatest treasure? Write about it. Here is what one student wrote.

My greatest treasure is my mother.

When I was little, I often had bad dreams. When I woke up, my mother always held me and took me into the garden for a short time. Then I could fall back to sleep again.

My mother always told me that I was not like other little girls. She told me I was special. Maybe that was true, and maybe it wasn't. But my mother believed it was true.

Sometimes I try to imagine that I am not my mother's daughter but someone else's daughter. I can't imagine it. I can't imagine having a different mother. She is my greatest treasure.

Now write about your greatest treasure.

1. PRE-READING

Look at the picture and guess the answers to these questions.

- In what country was the picture taken?
- In what year was the picture taken?

Listen while your classmates tell their guesses. Then look in the answer key for the correct answers. Did the answers surprise you? Do you know anything about the Amish? If you do, tell the class what you know.

The Plain People

IT is still dark when Elizabeth wakes up. She gets out of bed and shivers when her feet touch the cold, bare floor. The bedroom is not heated, and it is so cold that she can see her breath. She quickly puts on her long dress, black apron, and black shoes. Then she hurries downstairs to the kitchen.

The only light in the kitchen comes from kerosene lamps; Elizabeth's husband lit the lamps earlier, before he went out to milk the cows. Elizabeth puts a few pieces of wood into the stove and starts the fire. Then she begins to prepare a big breakfast for herself, her husband, and their six children. It is the beginning of a typical day for Elizabeth.

Although Elizabeth's day will be typical, her life is certainly not typical of life in the United States in the 1990s. Elizabeth belongs to a religious group known as the Amish. The Amish are often called the "Plain People" because they live and dress very simply. Their homes have no carpets on the floors, no pictures on the walls, and no soft, comfortable furniture. The men wear dark pants with white or blue shirts, and the women wear long dresses in dark colors. The women never wear makeup or jewelry.

The Amish have a saying: "The old way is the best way." Although the Amish accept some new ideas—they use new medicines, for example—their way of life has not changed much in 300 years. They do not use electricity, so Amish homes have no electric lights, no TVs, and no kitchen appliances like refrigerators. The Amish don't own telephones, either. They ride in buggies pulled by horses, and they speak German, the language that the first Amish people spoke.

The first Amish people lived in Germany and Switzerland. They were called Amish because their leader was Jacob Amman. The Amish were persecuted in Europe, so around 1700 they came to the New World. They settled in what is now the state of Pennsylvania.

Most of the Amish still live in Pennsylvania, although there are large communities in other states, too. All Amish, no matter where they live, have similar beliefs.

The Amish believe that life in the countryside is best. Almost all Amish live on farms. Amish farmers do not use modern machinery, yet their farms are successful because the Amish work hard and take good care of their land and animals. Their farms are always small. The Amish think it is wrong to have more land or more money than they need to live. A few years ago some Amish farmers discovered oil on their land. Was there a lot of oil under the ground, or just a little? The Amish farmers didn't want to know. They immediately sold their land and moved away, without telling anyone about the oil. They didn't want to be rich.

The Amish, who are Christians, believe they should follow the peaceful example of Jesus. Amish men will not fight in wars or serve in the army. They will not even wear coats with buttons, because military uniforms often have large gold or silver buttons.

The Amish will not buy insurance of any kind. When there is trouble, they help one another. If an Amish farmer gets sick, relatives and neighbors will milk his cows, plant his fields, and harvest his crops. If a barn burns down, as many as 200 men will come and build a new barn in one day.

The Amish are not allowed to marry people who are not Amish. That has caused a peculiar problem. The 500 or so Amish who came to the New World in the 1700s had about 40 last names. The 100,000 Amish who live in the United States today are the descendants of those people—and have the same 40 last names. In one school in Pennsylvania, 95 percent of the students—and their teacher—have the last name "Stolzfus." The Amish custom of choosing first names from the Bible adds to the problem. In one small Amish community there are 11 men named Daniel Miller!

To avoid confusion, the Amish give nicknames to people who have the same name. Some nicknames have an obvious explanation: "Chicken Dan" sells chickens, for example; "Curly Dan" has curly hair. But what about "Gravy Dan"? How did he get his nickname? At dinner one evening this Dan wanted to pour some cream into his coffee. He reached for the pitcher of cream but took the pitcher of gravy by mistake and poured gravy into his coffee. Ever since that evening, his nickname has been "Gravy Dan."

People are curious about the lives of Amish like Elizabeth and Gravy Dan. Every year thousands of tourists visit the part of Pennsylvania where most Amish live. They take pictures of the black buggies and the plain white houses. They watch Amish children as they walk to school and Amish men as they work in their fields. Most Amish are not happy about the tourists, but they tolerate them. Perhaps the Amish understand that the tourists want to experience, at least for a few days, the quieter, simpler Amish way of life.

2. VOCABULARY

A. LOOKING AT THE STORY

Which words have the same meaning as the words in the story? Circle the letter of the correct answer.

1. Elizabeth shivers when her feet touch the cold, *bare floor*.
   - **a.** floor that is not covered with a carpet
   - **b.** floor that is painted white

2. They do not use electricity, so Amish people have no kitchen *appliances* like refrigerators.
   - **a.** machines run by electricity and used in the house
   - **b.** furniture made out of wood and used in the house

3. *The Amish were persecuted* in Europe, so they came to the New World.
   - **a.** People didn't like them and were cruel to them
   - **b.** People liked them and were friendly to them

4. They *settled* in what is now the state of Pennsylvania.
   - **a.** found a new leader
   - **b.** came to live

5. There are large Amish *communities* in other states, too.
   - **a.** groups of people who left their countries because of politics
   - **b.** groups of people who live together

6. All Amish have similar *beliefs*.
   - **a.** objects that are important to them
   - **b.** ideas that they think are true

7. Amish men will not fight in wars. They will not even wear coats with buttons because *military uniforms* often have large gold or silver buttons.
   - **a.** the clothes worn by schoolchildren
   - **b.** the clothes worn by soldiers

8. If an Amish farmer gets sick, relatives and neighbors will *harvest his crops*.
   - **a.** pick the fruit, vegetables, and grain that he grows
   - **b.** bring him the medicine and other things that he needs

9. If a *barn* burns down, as many as 200 men will come and build a new barn in one day.
   - **a.** a house that is made of wood and built by hand
   - **b.** a building where a farmer keeps his crops and animals

10. The Amish are not allowed to marry people who are not Amish. That has caused a *peculiar* problem.
    - **a.** big
    - **b.** strange

11. A man took a pitcher of *gravy* by mistake and poured the gravy into his coffee.
    - **a.** a drink made with lemons, water, and sugar
    - **b.** a sauce for meat and potatoes

12. Most Amish are not happy about the tourists, but they *tolerate them*.
    - **a.** allow them to come
    - **b.** make them pay

B. LOOKING AT A NEW CONTEXT

Read the sentences. Then write the correct word on the line.

bare   appliance   tolerate

1. You can buy a microwave oven at an _____ store.

2. Usually I wear shoes, but when I am at the beach, my feet are _____.

3. I don't like cigarette smoke, but when my cousin comes to visit, I let him smoke in my

   house. I like my cousin, so I _____ the cigarette smoke.

Now make your own examples for these words:

bare	settle	military uniform	peculiar
appliance	community	harvest crops	gravy
persecute	belief	barn	tolerate

First, form small groups. One student in each group is the "teacher." The "teacher" will write each word on a separate small piece of paper, fold the papers, and give one to each person in the group. The "teacher" will take a word, too. Hold your paper so that no one can see your word. Make up a little story for the word like the ones above. (Be careful not to say your word.) Your classmates will listen to your story and try to guess which word you have. Then listen to your classmates' stories and try to guess which words they have.

3. COMPREHENSION/READING SKILLS

A. UNDERSTANDING THE MAIN IDEAS

What information is *not* in the story? Draw a line through the information.

1. Elizabeth
   a. sleeps in a bedroom that is not heated.
   b. wears a long dress, black apron, and black shoes.
   c. ~~has two sons.~~
   d. cooks on a wood stove.

2. The Amish
   a. are a religious group also called the "Plain People."
   b. live and dress very simply.
   c. live in California.
   d. believe that "the old way is the best way."

3. The first Amish people
   a. spoke French.
   b. were led by Jacob Amman.
   c. were persecuted in Europe.
   d. came to the New World around 1700.

4. Some Amish beliefs are:
   a. Life in the countryside is best.
   b. Follow the peaceful example of Jesus.
   c. Do not buy insurance.
   d. Do not work on Mondays.

B. UNDERSTANDING SUPPORTING DETAILS

Find the best way to complete each sentence. Write the letter of your answer on the line.

1. _____ Elizabeth's life is not typical of life in the United States in the 1990s. For example,

2. _____ The Amish dress very simply. For example,

3. _____ The Amish way of life has not changed much in 300 years. For example,

4. _____ The Amish help one another when there is trouble. For example,

5. _____ Some nicknames have an obvious explanation. For example,

a. they still speak German, the language that the first Amish people spoke.

b. "Chicken Dan" sells chickens and "Curly Dan" has curly hair.

c. she cooks on a wood stove.

d. if a barn burns down, as many as 200 men will come and build a new barn in a day.

e. the women wear long dresses in dark colors.

4. DISCUSSION

A. Think about these questions. Discuss your answers with your classmates.

1. The Amish have rules for living and dressing. Are there any religious groups in your native country that have special rules for living and dressing? Tell your classmates about them.
2. Could you live the way the Amish live? Could you live without electricity, without a car, and without a telephone?
3. Some Amish beliefs are: It is wrong to have more money than you need; never fight in wars; help one another when there is trouble. What do you think about these beliefs? Do you agree with them?
4. There is confusion because many Amish have the same last name. Are there some last names that many people in your native country have? What are the names?
5. The Amish give one another nicknames. Do you have a nickname? What is it? Is there a story behind your nickname, like the story of "Gravy Dan"?

B. Write about a religion you know by answering the questions in the chart on page 73. Then ask a classmate the questions and write your classmate's answers in the chart.

	YOU	YOUR CLASSMATE
1. Which religion do you know the most about?		
2. Where does this religion get its name?		
3. Does this religion have many different groups? If so, what are some of them called?		
4. Is there a holy book? What is it called?		
5. Is any day of the week special? Which day? What do people do on that day?		
6. Which religious holiday is most important? What does the holiday celebrate? What do people do on that holiday?		
7. Are there any rules about food?		
8. Are there any rules about clothing?		
9. What does this religion say happens to people after they die?		

5. WRITING

Write about one of the world's religions. Use the information you wrote in Exercise 4B, or use the information your classmate gave you. Here is what one student wrote.

The Mormon religion is a Christian religion that Joseph Smith began about 150 years ago. Most Mormons live in the United States, in the state of Utah.

Mormons have a lot of rules. They don't drink alcohol. They also don't drink coffee, tea, cola, or any drink that has caffeine in it. They must pay the church 10 percent of their income.

In the Mormon church there are no paid priests or ministers. People volunteer to work as ministers.

Years ago Mormon men had more than one wife. The Mormons' neighbors and the U.S. government didn't like that, and there was a lot of trouble. But today Mormon men have just one wife.

Now write about one of the world's religions.

1. PRE-READING

Think about these questions. Discuss your answers with your classmates.

- Do you know of any old person who died soon after an important event, like a holiday or birthday?
- Do you think that people can control the time of their own deaths?

Postponing Death

YINLAN looked at the people sitting around the table and smiled contentedly. Everyone in her family was there—her children, her grandchildren, and her new great-grandson, just one month old. Her whole family had come to celebrate the Harvest Moon Festival.

Yinlan had grown up in China, but she and her family now lived in San Francisco, California. Although they lived in the United States, Yinlan's family celebrated the Harvest Moon Festival just as Yinlan had in China. At the time of the full moon in August or September, her family gathered at her house for dinner. After dinner they ate moon cakes, a special round cookie. Then, if the sky was clear, they always walked outside to admire the full moon.

Tonight there was not a cloud in the sky, and the full moon shone brightly. Yinlan suggested that they all go outside. Her grandson helped her up from her chair. As Yinlan and her grandson walked toward the door, she held on to his arm and leaned against him for support. Yinlan was 86 years old. She had not been well the past few months, and her family noticed that she seemed weak.

Two days after the Harvest Moon Festival, Yinlan died peacefully in her sleep. Her family was sad but at the same time grateful. They felt happy that they had been able to celebrate the Harvest Moon Festival with her one last time. Everyone said it was remarkable that Yinlan had died just two days after the holiday.

Actually, the timing of Yinlan's death was not remarkable at all. Recently sociologists studied the death rate among elderly Chinese women in California. They discovered that the death rate drops 35 percent before the Harvest Moon Festival and then rises 35 percent: Each year there are fewer deaths than usual the week before the festival and more deaths than usual the week after. Sociologists believe that these changes in the death rate show the mind's power over the body. The Harvest Moon Festival, when families gather, is important to elderly Chinese women. Apparently some women are able to postpone their deaths so that they can celebrate the festival one last time.

Sociologists also studied the death rate of elderly Jewish men around the time of Passover, a Jewish holiday. They discovered the same phenomenon. During the week before Passover, the death rate among elderly Jewish men drops 24 percent. The week after Passover, the death rate rises 24 percent.

Passover is a Jewish religious holiday that is a family holiday as well. On the first two days of Passover, families gather in their homes for a ceremony. They sit around a table to share a special meal and to listen to the story of Passover. Traditionally, the oldest man in the family sits at the head of the table and reads the story. It is an important event for elderly Jewish men—so important that some men postpone their deaths until after Passover.

The idea that people can postpone the time of their deaths is not new. Many families tell stories of a relative who held on to life until after an important event. They tell of a grandmother who died after the birth of a grandchild, a grandfather who died after his 92nd birthday party. The stories people tell, however, are just that: stories. They are not proof that people can postpone their deaths. The sociologists' work is important because the sociologists studied facts, not stories. The facts—the drop and rise in death rates—prove that people really can postpone their deaths.

One famous person who may have postponed his death was Thomas Jefferson. Thomas Jefferson wrote the Declaration of Independence, one of the most important U.S. documents. The Declaration of Independence was signed on July 4, 1776. Thomas Jefferson died exactly 50 years later, on July 4, 1826. He died after asking his doctor, "Is it the Fourth?"

Historians have always thought that Jefferson's death on the Fourth of July was a remarkable coincidence. It now seems quite possible that the timing of Jefferson's death was no coincidence at all.

2. VOCABULARY

A. LOOKING AT THE STORY

Which words have the same meaning as the words in the story? Circle the letter of your answer.

1. Yinlan looked at the people sitting around the table and smiled *contentedly*.
   a. nervously
   b. happily

2. Yinlan's family celebrated the Harvest Moon Festival *just* as Yinlan had in China.
   a. exactly
   b. almost

3. Her family *gathered* at her house for dinner.
   a. came together
   b. cooked

4. Her family was sad, but at the same time *grateful*.
   a. not surprised
   b. thankful

5. It was *remarkable* that Yinlan had died just two days after the holiday.
   a. unusual; surprising
   b. sad; depressing

6. Sociologists studied *the death rate* among elderly Chinese women in California.
   a. the number of deaths compared to the number of people
   b. the number of people who die in a foreign country

7. The death rate *drops* 35 percent before the Harvest Moon Festival.
   a. goes up
   b. goes down

8. The death rate *rises* 35 percent after the festival.
   a. goes up
   b. goes down

9. *Apparently* some women are able to postpone their deaths.
   a. It seems that
   b. It is lucky that

10. Sociologists who studied the death rate of elderly Jewish men around the time of Passover discovered the same *phenomenon*.
    a. fact or event that is unusual and interesting
    b. holiday that is celebrated by families

11. Some Jewish men *postpone their deaths until after Passover*.
    a. wait until after Passover to die
    b. hope that they will not die until after Passover

12. The Declaration of Independence is one of the most important U.S. *documents*.
    a. buildings
    b. papers

13. Historians thought that Jefferson's death on the Fourth of July was a *coincidence*.
    a. an event that makes people feel sad
    b. two events that accidentally happen at the same time

B. LOOKING AT SPECIAL EXPRESSIONS

Find the best way to complete each sentence. Write the letter of your answer on the line.

to grow up = to change from a child to a man or woman

1. _____ Yinlan now lives in the United States, but

2. _____ When the little girl grows up,

3. _____ Because he grew up on a farm,

a. he knows how to take care of animals.

b. she wants to be a doctor.

c. she grew up in China.

3. COMPREHENSION/READING SKILLS

A. UNDERSTANDING THE MAIN IDEAS

What information is *not* in the story? Draw a line through the information.

1. Yinlan
   a. celebrated the Harvest Moon Festival with her family.
   b. was 86 years old.
   c. died two days after the Harvest Moon Festival.
   d. lived in a small apartment in San Francisco.

2. Sociologists
   a. studied the death rate among elderly Chinese women in San Francisco.
   b. believe that Chinese women live long because they eat a healthy diet.
   c. discovered that there are fewer deaths before the Harvest Moon Festival and more deaths after it.
   d. believe that the changes in the death rate show the mind's power over the body.

3. What happens during Passover?
   a. Families gather in their homes for a ceremony.
   b. Families share a special meal.
   c. Parents give their children gifts of money and chocolate.
   d. The oldest man in the family reads the story of Passover.

4. Sociologists
   a. studied the death rate of elderly Jewish men around the time of Passover.
   b. discovered that their death rate drops 24 percent before Passover.
   c. discovered that their death rate rises 24 percent after Passover.
   d. went to Jewish homes to learn how Jews celebrate Passover.

5. The sociologists' work on death rates
   a. is important.
   b. was a study of facts, not stories.
   c. was done in 1989.
   d. proves that people really can postpone their deaths.

6. Thomas Jefferson
   a. wrote the Declaration of Independence.
   b. helped plan the city of Washington, D.C.
   c. died on July 4, 1826—exactly 50 years after the Declaration of Independence was signed.
   d. may have postponed his death.

B. SCANNING FOR INFORMATION

The underlined information is not correct. Find the correct information in the story and write it. Work quickly; try to complete the exercise in three minutes or less.

1. Yinlan had grown up in China, but she and her family now lived in <u>Los Angeles</u>, California.

2. <u>Five years ago</u> sociologists studied the death rate among elderly Chinese women in California.

3. They discovered that the death rate drops <u>24</u> percent before the Harvest Moon Festival.

4. Sociologists also studied the death rate of elderly Jewish men at the time of <u>Hanukkah</u>, a Jewish holiday.

5. During the week before Passover, the death rate drops <u>23</u> percent.

6. On the first <u>three</u> days of Passover, families gather in their homes for a ceremony.

7. One famous person who may have postponed his death was <u>William</u> Jefferson.

8. Jefferson was the author of the <u>Bill of Rights</u>, one of the most important U.S. documents.

9. The Declaration of Independence was signed on July 4, <u>1774</u>.

10. Jefferson died exactly <u>40</u> years later.

4. DISCUSSION

Think about these questions. Discuss your answers with your classmates.

1. One question in the pre-reading exercise was: "Do you think people can control the time of their own deaths?" After reading the story, is your answer to that question still the same, or has it changed?
2. After reading "Postponing Death," do you now think someone you know may have postponed his or her death? Tell your classmates about it.
3. Do you think the mind has power over the body? Do you think, for example, that people can control whether or not they get sick or feel pain?
4. The Harvest Moon Festival is important to the Chinese, and Passover is important to Jews. Is there a holiday that is important to you—so important that you would postpone your death to experience it one last time?
5. Thomas Jefferson died on July 4, 1826—50 years after the Declaration of Independence was signed. That was a remarkable coincidence. Do you know of a remarkable coincidence? Tell your classmates about it.

5. WRITING

A. The sociologists believe that their studies show the mind's power over the body. Have you ever used your mind to control your body? Do you know a story that shows that the mind can control the body? Write a paragraph or two. Here is what one student wrote.

I read a story in the newspaper about an elderly woman who was dying in a hospital. She asked the doctor to call her only son because she wanted to see him one last time. But before her son arrived, the woman's heart stopped beating. The doctor met the woman's son in the lobby of the hospital and told him that his mother had died. When the son went to his mother's room and began to cry, a machine connected to the woman showed that the woman's heart was beating again. The woman opened her eyes, looked at her son, and smiled. A few minutes later she peacefully left the world again.

Now write your paragraph(s).

B. Write about a holiday that is important to you. How do you celebrate it? Here is what one student wrote.

When I was a little girl, my favorite day was March 3. That is when people in Japan celebrate Hinamatsuri, a holiday for girls. The girls dress dolls in beautiful dresses called kimonos and display the dolls. Girls usually get the dolls ready about a week before the holiday. (People say that girls who dress their dolls early get married early, but that wasn't true for me! I always dressed my dolls early, but I am 26 years old and not married.) The first time a girl celebrates Hinamatsuri, her relatives come to her house. Everybody drinks "Shirozake," a special drink, and eats sweets we call "Sakuramochi." The next day, on March 4, the girls put their dolls away. I always felt a little sad when Hinamatsuri was over and it was time to put my dolls away.

Now write about a holiday that is important to you.

1. PRE-READING

Imagine that after shopping, you return to your car, which is parked in a parking lot. It is 9 o'clock at night, and there are only a few people in the parking lot. When you get into your car, a man jumps up from the back seat, holds a gun to your head, and says, "Drive!" What would you do? Check an answer, or write your own answer. Then compare your answer with those of your classmates.

I would

1. _____ scream and yell to get the attention of the people in the parking lot.

2. _____ try to grab the gun.

3. _____ tell the man I'll drive him where he wants to go, but then drive to a police station.

4. _____ drive where the man tells me to go.

5. _____ _____

An Unexpected Adventure

ONE summer afternoon Jean and Clothilde Lestarquit, an elderly couple, visited their daughter at her home in Lille, France. A few minutes before six o'clock, the Lestarquits decided to leave. They said goodbye to their daughter, walked to their car, and got in. They expected a quiet, uneventful ride home. The ride, however, was anything but quiet and uneventful.

Mr. Lestarquit was about to start the car when a gunman jumped up from the back seat. He held a gun to Mr. Lestarquit's head. "Drive me to Paris!" he demanded.

"All right," Mr. Lestarquit replied. "I'll drive you anywhere you want to go. But first let my wife out of the car."

The gunman agreed to let Mrs. Lestarquit go. After she was safely out of the car, Mr. Lestarquit started the engine, pulled away from the curb, and drove down the street. He was driving slowly, but his mind was racing. Unarmed and 81 years old, he knew he could not fight the gunman. He knew he needed help. Where were the police? As he drove through each intersection, he looked up and down the side streets, hoping to spot a police car. There was none in sight. "Just my luck," he thought. "If I were speeding, there would be a police car on every corner."

Suddenly Mr. Lestarquit realized how he could attract the attention of the police. He pushed his foot down on the accelerator of his Mercedes, and the car sped forward. "What are you doing?" shouted the gunman. "Avoiding the police," Mr. Lestarquit lied. "I thought I saw a police car back there."

Mr. Lestarquit began driving like a madman. He drove 60 miles an hour on side streets, ran red lights, and drove the wrong way on one-way streets. On two-way streets he drove on the wrong side of the road. Not one police officer saw him.

Obviously, Mr. Lestarquit's plan was not working. He needed a new plan. But what? Suddenly he remembered that the Lille police station was only a few blocks away. "All right," he thought. "If I can't bring the police to my car, I'll bring my car to the police."

He turned a corner and saw the police station ahead. Immediately his heart sank. There was a courtyard in front of the police station, and the two large doors that led to the courtyard were closed. Mr. Lestarquit hesitated for a moment. Then he pushed the accelerator to the floor and steered straight for the doors.

The car crashed through the doors and stopped in the courtyard. Mr. Lestarquit yelled, "Help! He's going to kill me!" Then he reached back to grab the man's gun. Just as he grabbed it, the gunman pulled the trigger. The bullet grazed Mr. Lestarquit's hand and went through the windshield. Before the gunman could pull the trigger again, Mr. Lestarquit opened the car door and fell to the ground. Officers from the police station, who had come running when they heard the crash, quickly captured the gunman. It was 6:30 P.M.— exactly 35 minutes since the Lestarquits had left their daughter's house on a quiet street in Lille.

It seemed to Jean Lestarquit that for those 35 minutes he had stepped out of reality and into an action movie. There were so many things action movies have—a gunman, a hero, a speeding car, and a car crash. Fortunately for Jean Lestarquit, there was one more thing most action movies have: a happy ending.

2. VOCABULARY

A. LOOKING AT THE STORY

Think about the story and answer the questions.

1. Mr. Lestarquit *pulled away from the curb*. Is the car pulling away from the curb in picture *a* or in picture *b*?

   a.   b.

2. Mr. Lestarquit was *unarmed*. Did he have a gun?

3. Are *side streets* usually narrow or wide?

4. Mr. Lestarquit was hoping to *spot* a police car, but there was none *in sight*. Did Mr. Lestarquit see a police car?

5. Do drivers who *speed* drive fast or slowly?

6. Do drivers push down on the *accelerator* when they want to stop or go faster?

7. When drivers *run red lights*, do they stop at the red lights or continue driving?

8. When Mr. Lestarquit saw the police station, *his heart sank*. Did he feel happy or sad?

9. Which building has a *courtyard*—the building in picture *a* or the building in picture *b*?

   a.    b.

10. After the bullet *grazed* Mr. Lestarquit's hand, was his hand hurt a little or hurt very badly?

_____

11. Is a *windshield* made of glass or metal?

_____

12. Does a *captured* gunman go home or go to the police station?

_____

B. LOOKING AT SPECIAL EXPRESSIONS

Find the best way to complete each sentence. Write the letter of your answer on the line.

anything but = not at all

1. _____ The ride, however,

2. _____ That bridge

3. _____ That restaurant

a. is anything but safe.

b. is anything but inexpensive.

c. was anything but quiet and uneventful.

about to = to be ready to

4. _____ Mr. Lestarquit was about to start the car

5. _____ We were about to play tennis

6. _____ I was about to buy a jacket for $60

d. when a gunman jumped up from the floor of the back seat.

e. when I saw a nicer one for $50.

f. when it started to rain.

3. COMPREHENSION/READING SKILLS

A. UNDERSTANDING TIME RELATIONSHIPS

What information is *not* correct? Draw a line through it.

1. About six o'clock Mr. and Mrs. Lestarquit
   a. decided to leave their daughter's house.
   b. arrived home safely.
   c. said goodbye to their daughter.
   d. walked to their car and got in.

2. Mr. Lestarquit was about to start the car when a gunman
   a. jumped up from the back seat.
   b. held a gun to Mr. Lestarquit's head.
   c. demanded that Mr. Lestarquit drive him to Paris.
   d. pulled the trigger.

(Continued on next page.)

3. After Mrs. Lestarquit was out of the car, Mr. Lestarquit
   a. started the engine.
   b. pulled away from the curb.
   c. got into his car.
   d. tried to spot a police car.

4. After Mr. Lestarquit realized how he could attract the attention of the police, he
   a. drove 60 miles an hour on side streets.
   b. ran red lights.
   c. drove the wrong way on one-way streets.
   d. said, "Let my wife out of the car."

5. After Mr. Lestarquit crashed through the doors leading to the courtyard,
   a. the car stopped.
   b. he grabbed the gun.
   c. the gunman pulled the trigger.
   d. the gunman shouted, "What are you doing?"

B. UNDERSTANDING DETAILS

Read the sentences from the story. One word in each sentence is not correct. Find the word and cross it out. Write the correct word.

1. Jean and Clothilde Lestarquit, an elderly couple, visited their daughter at her home in Lille, Spain.

2. They said goodbye to their daughter and walked to their bicycles.

3. Mr. Lestarquit was about to start the car when a policeman jumped up from the back seat.

4. "Drive me to Barcelona!" the man demanded.

5. Mr. Lestarquit said, "I'll drive you anywhere you want to go, but first let my daughter out of the car."

Now copy three sentences from the story, but change one word in each sentence so that the information is not correct. Give your sentences to a classmate. Your classmate will find the incorrect word in each sentence, cross it out, and write the correct word. When your classmate is finished, check the corrections.

6. _____

   _____

7. _____

   _____

8. _____

   _____

4. DISCUSSION

A. Think about these questions. Discuss your answers with your classmates.

1. Do you think Mr. Lestarquit was brave or foolish? Why?
2. What would you have done if you had been in his place?

B. With a partner or in small groups, talk about what you would do in the following dangerous situations.

1. You are walking down the street when suddenly a big dog runs toward you. The dog is barking.
2. You are walking down a busy street in a big city. A man walks up to you and says, "Give me your money!" He has a knife.
3. It is 11 o'clock at night. You are home alone watching TV. There is a knock at the door. You aren't expecting anyone.
4. You come home late at night. The door to your house or apartment is open. You are sure you locked the door when you left the house. You live alone.
5. You and a friend go to a party in your friend's car. Your friend drinks beer at the party. When it is time to go home, you realize that your friend has had too much to drink.

5. WRITING

A. Write a police report. Imagine that you were one of the police officers at the Lille police station. After capturing the gunman, you asked Mr. Lestarquit what happened and then wrote down what he told you. What is your report?

B. Have you ever had an experience like Jean Lestarquit's? Have you ever been in a dangerous situation where you had to decide what to do? Write about your experience. Here is what one student wrote.

> When I was in high school I was in a dangerous situation almost every day.
> One day after school a group of boys surrounded my friends and me. There were about 20 of them. There were three of us. My friends and I had to decide whether to fight or run. We decided to fight. We started to fight, and then fortunately some university students came along and separated us.
> There were other dangerous situations, too, but that is one I remember very well.

Now write about your experience.

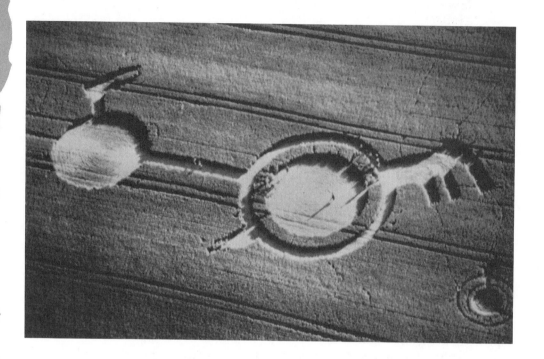

1. PRE-READING

A. The people in the picture are standing in a field of wheat in England. What do you think made the circles in the wheat? Check one or more answers, or write your own answer. Then compare your answers with those of your classmates.

1. _____ a tractor or other farm machine

2. _____ animals

3. _____ beings from outer space

4. _____ a helicopter

5. _____ the wind

6. _____ people who walked on the wheat

7. _____ _____

B. Have you read or heard about these circles? Where did you read or hear about them? Tell your classmates what you know about them.

An Unsolved Mystery

IN the summer of 1978 an English farmer named Ian Stevens was driving his tractor through a field of wheat when he discovered something strange. Some of his wheat was lying flat on the ground. The flattened wheat formed a circle about six meters across. Around this circle were four smaller circles of flattened wheat. The five circles were in a formation like five dots on dice.

Three years later a farmer who lived nearby discovered similar circles in one of his fields. These circles were larger—nearly 15 meters across. That same year, yet another English farmer discovered three circles of flattened wheat on his land—one large circle between two small circles.

During the following years, farmers in England found the mysterious circles in their fields more and more often. In 1987 they discovered 50 circles; in 1988, 98 circles; and in 1989, 270 circles.

The circles are called "crop circles" because they appear in fields of grain—usually wheat or corn. The grain in the circles lies flat on the ground but is never broken; it continues to grow horizontally, and farmers can later harvest it. Farmers always discover the crop circles in the morning, so the circles probably form at night. They appear only in the months from May to September. What causes the crop circles?

At first, people suspected that the circles were a hoax. They thought that teenagers were making them as a joke, or that farmers were making them to attract tourists. (In fact, in 1991, two men said they made the circles themselves, but many scientists don't believe them.) To prove that the circles were a hoax, people tried to copy them: they tried to make circles exactly like the ones the farmers had found. They couldn't do it. They couldn't enter a field of grain without leaving tracks, and they couldn't flatten the grain without breaking it. The crop circles are apparently not a hoax.

Many people believe that beings from outer space are making the circles. Some think that the beings are trying to communicate with us from far away and that the crop circles are messages from them. Others believe that the beings have actually landed on earth and that the circles are marks left by their spaceships. Several times people reported seeing strange flying objects near fields where crop circles later appeared.

Scientists who have studied the crop circles say they're not sure what causes them. They have suggested several theories. For example, some scientists say that "microbursts" of wind create the circles. A microburst is a downward rush of cool air—the same downward rush of air that sometimes causes an airplane to crash. Other scientists say that forces *within* the earth cause the circles to appear. There is one problem with all the scientific theories. Crop circles often appear in formations, like the five-dot formation that Ian Stevens found. It is hard to believe that any natural force could create those formations. And recently farmers have discovered not only circles, but rectangles, triangles, and other shapes in their fields. Could any natural force create a perfect triangle in a field of grain?

In the summer of 1990 some scientists spent three weeks in the part of England where many circles have appeared. They had all the latest high-tech equipment. This equipment—worth 1.8 million dollars—recorded nothing. But one night, as the scientists were watching a field, crop circles formed in the field behind them. These circles are shown in the photograph. The scientists had neither seen nor heard anything.

When Ian Stevens discovered the crop circles on his land in 1978, he said, "It was just like something had landed in the field from the air and gone back up again. I don't know what to make of these things."

Crop circles have appeared not only in England, but in fields in Japan, the United States, the Soviet Union, and New Zealand. Experts from all over the world have studied them. What do the experts say about the crop circles? They say what Ian Stevens said: They don't know what to make of these things.

2. VOCABULARY

A. LOOKING AT THE STORY

Which words or picture has the same meaning as the words in the story? Circle the letter of your answer.

1. The five circles were in a formation like the five dots found on *dice*.

   a.

   b.

2. These circles were larger—*nearly* 15 meters across.
   a. more than
   b. almost

3. That same year, *yet another* English farmer discovered three circles of flattened wheat on his land.
   a. the same
   b. one more

4. During the following years, farmers in England found the *mysterious* circles in their fields more and more often.
   a. not easy to hear or see
   b. not easy to understand or explain

5. The grain continues to grow *horizontally*.
   a. _____
   b. _____

6. Some people suspected that the circles were *a hoax*.
   a. a trick
   b. an experiment

7. They couldn't enter a field of grain without leaving *tracks*.
   a. machines that farmers use
   b. marks made by people, animals, or cars

8. Scientists who have studied the crop circles have suggested several *theories*.
   a. ideas that haven't been proven
   b. scientific books about wind

9. It is hard to believe that any natural force could *create* such perfect formations.
   a. find
   b. make

10. The scientists had all the latest high-tech *equipment*.
    a. things they needed to watch the field
    b. money they were paid to watch the field

11. *The scientists had neither seen nor heard anything.*
    a. Some scientists had seen something; other scientists had heard something.
    b. The scientists had not seen anything; they had not heard anything, either.

B. LOOKING AT SPECIAL EXPRESSIONS

Find the best way to complete each sentence. Write the letter of your answer on the line.

the latest = the newest; the most recent

1. _____ The scientists had

2. _____ Let's go into this store—

3. _____ She always listens to the radio

a. all the latest high-tech equipment.

b. because she wants to hear the latest news.

c. they have all the latest fashions.

to know what to make of = to understand

4. _____ Ian Stevens said,

5. _____ He's been behaving strangely;

6. _____ When our teacher told us, "You'll be surprised when you see the test,"

d. nobody knows what to make of his behavior.

e. "I don't know what to make of these things."

f. we didn't know what to make of her statement.

3. COMPREHENSION/READING SKILLS

A. UNDERSTANDING THE MAIN IDEAS

What information is *not* in the story? Draw a line through the information.

1. The circle of wheat that Ian Stevens found in 1978
   a. was about six meters across.
   b. was lying flat on the ground.
   c. had four smaller circles around it.
   d. ~~was made by his tractor.~~

2. The crop circles
   a. are making farmers in England rich.
   b. probably form at night.
   c. usually appear in fields of wheat or corn.
   d. appear only from May to September.

3. The grain inside the circles
   a. always lies flat on the ground.
   b. is never broken.
   c. can be eaten only by farm animals.
   d. can be harvested.

4. People said that the circles were made by
   a. teenagers who wanted to play a joke.
   b. farmers who wanted to attract tourists.
   c. animals who slept in the fields at night.
   d. beings from outer space.

(Continued on next page.)

5. Scientists think the circles might be caused by
    a. microbursts of wind.
    b. helicopters.
    c. forces within the earth.

6. The problem with the scientific theories is that it is hard to believe that any natural force could
    a. create formations like the five-dot formation.
    b. create shapes like rectangles and triangles.
    c. create crop circles during the night.

7. In the summer of 1990 some scientists
    a. spent three weeks in the part of England where many circles have appeared.
    b. had all the latest high-tech equipment.
    c. did not see or hear anything when the crop circles in the photograph formed.
    d. thought of some important new theories about crop circles.

B. SCANNING FOR INFORMATION

The underlined information is not correct. Find the correct information in the story and write it. Work quickly; try to complete this exercise in three minutes or less.

1. In the summer of 1978 an English farmer named Ian <u>Smith</u> was driving his tractor through a field of wheat when he discovered something strange.

2. The flattened wheat formed a circle about <u>three</u> meters across.

3. Around this circle were <u>five</u> smaller circles of flattened wheat.

4. <u>Two</u> years later another farmer who lived nearby discovered similar circles in one of his fields.

5. These circles were larger—nearly <u>14</u> meters across.

6. That same year yet another English farmer discovered <u>two</u> circles of flattened wheat on his land.

7. In 1987 farmers in England discovered 50 circles; in 1988, <u>108</u> circles; and in 1989, 270 circles.

8. In the summer of 1990 some scientists spent <u>four</u> weeks in the part of England where many circles have appeared.

9. The equipment—worth <u>1.7</u> million dollars—recorded nothing.

10. But one <u>morning</u>, as the scientists were watching a field, crop circles formed in the field behind them.

4. DISCUSSION

What do you think causes the crop circles? Check the theory that you think is correct, or write your own theory.

Who or what is making the crop circles?

1. _____Teenagers

2. _____Farmers

3. _____Beings who are trying to communicate from outer space

4. _____Spaceships that have landed

5. _____Microbursts of wind

6. _____Forces within the earth

7. _____

Now work as a class and answer the questions.

1. How many students checked #1? How many checked #2? #3? #4? #5? #6? #7? What did the students who checked #7 write? Why did you check the theory you did? Which theory got the most checks?
2. People reported seeing unidentified flying objects (UFOs) near fields where crop circles later appeared. Many think the UFOs are spaceships. In your native country, do people sometimes report that they saw UFOs? What do you think about UFOs?
3. Perhaps you had read or heard about the crop circles before you read the story. Did the story give you any new or different information about the circles? Did it change your opinion about what causes them?

5. WRITING

A. What do you think causes the crop circles? Write about a theory that you think is correct.

B. Imagine that you are standing alone in a field in southern England when a spaceship lands. Beings from outer space get out of the spaceship. Write five or six questions that you would like to ask them.

Answer Key

UNIT 1

Vocabulary
A. Looking at the Story
1. They are usually happy.   **2.** Water goes through a garden hose.   **3.** Shoes are made of leather.   **4.** They stay together.   **5.** It is knives, forks, and spoons.   **6.** He has hair on his face.   **7.** They cut.   **8.** He walked quietly.   **9.** They are on windows.   **10.** She thought, "I had good luck."   **11.** Mary rarely misbehaves.   **12.** They kick with their feet.
B. Looking at a New Context
1. Fortunately   **2.** kick   **3.** leather

Comprehension/Reading Skills
A. Understanding the Main Ideas
1. d   **2.** b   **3.** b   **4.** a
B. Understanding Details
1. Korean/French   **2.** best/worst   **3.** 2000/2,000
4. good/bad   **5.** boy/girl

UNIT 2

Vocabulary
A. Looking at the Story
1. a   **2.** b   **3.** a   **4.** b   **5.** a   **6.** a   **7.** a   **8.** a
9. b   **10.** b   **11.** b   **12.** a
B. Looking at a New Context
1. blamed   **2.** connected   **3.** just

Comprehension/Reading Skills
A. Understanding the Main Ideas
1. d   **2.** c   **3.** b   **4.** a   **5.** d   **6.** a   **7.** b
B. Understanding Cause and Effect
1. c   **2.** a   **3.** d   **4.** b

UNIT 3

Vocabulary
A. Looking at the Story
1. a   **2.** a   **3.** a   **4.** b   **5.** b   **6.** a   **7.** a   **8.** b
9. b   **10.** a   **11.** b   **12.** a
B. Looking at a New Context
1. disappointed   **2.** enthusiastic   **3.** alike

Comprehension/Reading Skills
A. Understanding the Main Ideas
1. b   **2.** a   **3.** b   **4.** c   **5.** c   **6.** b   **7.** b
B. Understanding Supporting Details
1. c   **2.** e   **3.** a   **4.** d   **5.** b

UNIT 4

Vocabulary
A. Looking at the Story
1. They are adults.   **2.** Three children are born at the same time.   **3.** It is a long trip.   **4.** A horse and a donkey are the parents of a mule.   **5.** It is small and roughly built.   **6.** It is easy to see.   **7.** It does not permit birth control.   **8.** It is a home for children who have no parents.   **9.** They took the boys into their family.   **10.** She wants God to think about her age.
B. Looking at Special Expressions
1. c   **2.** b   **3.** a   **4.** f   **5.** d   **6.** e   **7.** h   **8.** i   **9.** g

Comprehension/Reading Skills
A. Understanding the Main Ideas
1. c   **2.** c   **3.** c   **4.** c   **5.** b   **6.** c
B. Scanning for Information
1. 30   **2.** 21   **3.** Argentina   **4.** Chile   **5.** two   **6.** triplets
7. 16   **8.** Colina   **9.** five   **10.** three

UNIT 5

Vocabulary
A. Looking at the Story
1. a   **2.** b   **3.** b   **4.** a   **5.** b   **6.** b   **7.** a   **8.** a
9. b   **10.** a
B. Looking at Special Expressions
1. c   **2.** a   **3.** b

Comprehension/Reading Skills
A. Understanding the Main Ideas
1. c   **2.** c   **3.** b   **4.** a   **5.** c   **6.** c
B. Understanding Supporting Details
1. d   **2.** c   **3.** a   **4.** b

UNIT 6

Vocabulary
A. Looking at the Story
1. a   **2.** a   **3.** a   **4.** a   **5.** a   **6.** b   **7.** b   **8.** b
9. b   **10.** a   **11.** a   **12.** b
B. Looking at a New Context
1. suspected   **2.** embraced   **3.** lanterns

Comprehension/Reading Skills
A. Understanding Cause and Effect
1. c   **2.** d   **3.** a   **4.** e   **5.** b
B. Understanding Time Relationships
1. 79   **2.** TODAY   **3.** 79   **4.** 1860s   **5.** 79   **6.** 79
7. 1860s   **8.** 79   **9.** 79   **10.** TODAY

UNIT 7

Vocabulary
A. Looking at the Story
1. a   **2.** a   **3.** b   **4.** a   **5.** a   **6.** a   **7.** a   **8.** b
9. b   **10.** b   **11.** a   **12.** b
B. Looking at Special Expressions
1. b   **2.** a   **3.** c   **4.** d   **5.** f   **6.** e   **7.** i   **8.** h   **9.** g
10. k   **11.** j   **12.** l   **13.** m   **14.** n   **15.** o

Comprehension/Reading Skills
A. Understanding Cause and Effect
1. b   **2.** a   **3.** d   **4.** e   **5.** c
B. Understanding Details
1. dollars/cents   **2.** train/bus   **3.** Washington/New York
4. driver/passenger   **5.** foot/shoulder

UNIT 8

Vocabulary
A. Looking at the Story
1. a   **2.** b   **3.** a   **4.** b   **5.** a   **6.** a   **7.** a   **8.** b
9. a   **10.** a   **11.** b   **12.** a
B. Looking at Special Expressions
1. b   **2.** a   **3.** c   **4.** d   **5.** f   **6.** e   **7.** i   **8.** g   **9.** h
10. k   **11.** j   **12.** l

Comprehension/Reading Skills
A. Understanding Cause and Effect
1. c **2.** e **3.** a **4.** d **5.** b
B. Understanding Details
1. paint/dust **2.** Rome/Paris **3.** new/old **4.** $30/$3
5. mathematics/geography

UNIT 9

Vocabulary
A. Looking at the Story
1. b **2.** b **3.** a **4.** a **5.** a **6.** a **7.** a **8.** b
9. a **10.** b **11.** b **12.** b
B. Looking at Special Expressions
1. c **2.** a **3.** b **4.** e **5.** f **6.** d **7.** h **8.** i **9.** g

Comprehension/Reading Skills
A. Understanding the Main Ideas
Children are usually not superstitious.   It is always a good idea
to take a numerologist's advice.   People who use purple towels
are silly.
B. Understanding Supporting Details
1. d **2.** e **3.** c **4.** a **5.** b

UNIT 10

Vocabulary
A. Looking at the Story
1. resort **2.** allowed **3.** bothers **4.** raising a family
5. situation **6.** a break **7.** admits **8.** hiking **9.** scenery
10. entire **11.** sip **12.** responsibilities
B. Looking at a New Context
1. allowed **2.** bothers **3.** sip

Comprehension/Reading Skills
A. Understanding the Main Ideas
1. b **2.** a **3.** b **4.** c **5.** c
B. Understanding Supporting Details
1. d **2.** b **3.** a **4.** c

UNIT 11

Vocabulary
A. Looking at the Story
1. They rob ships. **2.** It is gold, silver, and jewels. **3.** They
are used for digging. **4.** It is a type of wood. **5.** They are
surprised. **6.** They looked carefully. **7.** They made people
feel sure. **8.** They want to use money to make money.
9. They are machines that make holes. **10.** They brought
pumps to the island to take water out of the hole. **11.** They
collected the money. **12.** It is big.
B. Looking at Special Expressions
. b **2.** a **3.** c

Comprehension/Reading Skills
A. Understanding Time Relationships
1. c **2.** c **3.** d **4.** b **5.** c
B. Scanning for Information
. McGinnis **2.** oak **3.** The next day **4.** Two **5.** 13
. Eight **7.** evening **8.** 1850 **9.** five **10.** 20

UNIT 12

Pre-reading
the United States;   about 1980

Vocabulary
A. Looking at the Story
1. a **2.** a **3.** a **4.** b **5.** b **6.** b **7.** b **8.** a
. b **10.** b **11.** b **12.** a

B. Looking at a New Context
1. appliance **2.** bare **3.** tolerate

Comprehension/Reading Skills
A. Understanding the Main Ideas
1. c **2.** c **3.** a **4.** d
B. Understanding Supporting Details
1. c **2.** e **3.** a **4.** d **5.** b

UNIT 13

Vocabulary
A. Looking at the Story
1. b **2.** a **3.** a **4.** b **5.** a **6.** a **7.** b **8.** a
9. a **10.** a **11.** a **12.** b **13.** b
B. Looking at Special Expressions
1. c **2.** b **3.** a

Comprehension/Reading Skills
A. Understanding the Main Ideas
1. d **2.** b **3.** c **4.** d **5.** c **6.** b
B. Scanning for Information
1. San Francisco **2.** Recently **3.** 35 **4.** Passover
5. 24 **6.** two **7.** Thomas **8.** Declaration of Independence
9. 1776 **10.** 50

UNIT 14

Vocabulary
A. Looking at the Story
1. It is pulling away from the curb in picture a. **2.** No, he
didn't have a gun. **3.** They are usually narrow. **4.** No, he
didn't. **5.** They drive fast. **6.** They push down on the
accelerator when they want to go faster. **7.** They continue
driving. **8.** He felt sad. **9.** The building in picture a. has a
courtyard. **10.** His hand was hurt a little. **11.** It is made of
glass. **12.** He goes to the police station.
B. Looking at Special Expressions
1. c **2.** a **3.** b **4.** d **5.** f **6.** e

Comprehension/Reading Skills
A. Understanding Time Relationships
1. b **2.** d **3.** c **4.** d **5.** d
B. Understanding Details
1. Spain/France **2.** bicycles/car **3.** policeman/gunman
4. Barcelona/Paris **5.** daughter/wife

UNIT 15

Vocabulary
A. Looking at the Story
1. a **2.** b **3.** b **4.** b **5.** b **6.** a **7.** b **8.** a
9. b **10.** a **11.** b
B. Looking at Special Expressions
1. a **2.** c **3.** b **4.** e **5.** d **6.** f

Comprehension/Reading Skills
A. Understanding the Main Ideas
1. d **2.** a **3.** c **4.** c **5.** b **6.** c **7.** d
B. Scanning for Information
1. Stevens **2.** six **3.** four **4.** Three **5.** 15 **6.** three
7. 98 **8.** three **9.** 1.8 **10.** night

ACKNOWLEDGMENTS

I wish to thank:

- my husband, parents, and sisters for always being on the lookout for good true stories;
- my nephew Nathaniel Hajdu for faithfully sending the clippings;
- Joanne Dresner and Penny Laporte at Longman for their enthusiasm for this project;
- Randee Falk for her thoughtful editing;
- fellow teacher and fellow walker Nancy Hayward for her suggestions for the writing exercises;
- Cyrus Rowshan at the American Language Institute at IUP for teaching assignments that facilitated field-testing;
- my students at the American Language Institute at Indiana University of Pennsylvania for the examples for the vocabulary and writing exercises;
- Donald Gingrich for the newspaper articles about the Friendship Force's U.S.-Soviet exchange;
- E. David Luria, Patrice Reynolds, Gloria Greenbaum, Trudy Janke, Joe Parris, Kathy Dodson, Charles Cook, and many other members of The Friendship Force for sharing anecdotes, photos, and clippings;
- Anna Hughes Carone for the information about the stages of culture shock;
- Narrye Caldwell for information about acupuncture and alternative types of medicine;
- Jeff Korman at the Enoch Pratt Free Library, Baltimore, for information about the *bum/bomb* mixup;
- Cyrus Rowshan and Sharron Bassano for their accounts of ''misunderstandings'';
- John Shaughnessy at the *Indianapolis Star* for information about the map;
- Max Buten, one of the 13 members of the Friday the 13th Club, for sending photos;
- Mindy Geller at the Toyota Corporation for verifying the Toyoda/Toyota story;
- Ali Aghbar, Ray Thomas, and Geraldine Zalazar at IUP for relinquishing class time so that I could question their students about superstitions;
- Huisen Shi and Rong Liu for their descriptions of the Harvest Moon Festival and Don Eisen for his description of Passover;
- Marie Olsen for translating materials for ''An Unexpected Adventure'';
- Ron Lunardini, Malcolm Hayward, Al Novels, and the Campus Police at IUP for their help with the photography.

CREDITS

We wish to thank the following for permission to adapt material:

(for page 8) *The Design of Everyday Things* by Donald Norman. New York: Doubleday, 1990.

(for page 20) ''Supermom.'' The Associated Press, as reported in the *Pittsburgh Press*, 8 May 1988.

(for page 25) Discussion Exercise 4B (''Invisible Pictures'') is from *The Recipe Book* by Seth Lindstromberg, Longman, 1990.

(for page 44) ''Paris map may show man route to riches,'' by Jo Ellen Meyers Sharp, the *Indianapolis Star*, 17 August 1985.

(for page 56) The information on two-career couples and housework is from *The Second Shift: Inside the Two-Job Marriage* by Arlie Hochschild. Penguin/Viking, 1989.

(for page 62) ''The Secret of Oak Island,'' adaptation by permission of the National Geographic Society, copyright © June 1989, *World* magazine.

(for page 74) The statistics on the death rates of elderly Chinese women and elderly Jewish men are the findings of David Phillips as reported in *Lancet* (1988) and the *Journal of the American Medical Association* (1990).

(for page 80) ''A Lille, vraie-fausse prise d'otage dans la cour de la gendarmerie,'' *La Voix du Nord*, 8 August 1989.

The format for many of the discussion exercises was inspired by Irene Schoenberg's *Talk About Values*, Longman, 1989.

We wish to thank the following for providing us with photographs:

For cover and page 2, courtesy of *Weekly World News*; page 8, Tony Korody/*People* Weekly © 1989 The Time Inc. Magazine Co.; cover and page 14, courtesy of The Friendship Force; page 20, AP/Wide World Photos; page 26, Lou Mack/*Los Angeles Times*; page 32, Lou Battaglia/National Geographic Society; page 38, photo by Sandra Heyer; page 44, Rick Myers; page 50, photo by Sandra Heyer; page 56, Steve Schapiro/Gamma-Liaison; page 62, The Bettmann Archive; page 68, courtesy of the Pennsylvania Dutch Visitors Bureau; page 74, The Bettman Archive; page 80, Bernard Dublique; cover and page 86, AP/Wide World Photos.